dream. search. apply.

A FIELD GUIDE FOR
AN INSPIRED COLLEGE JOURNEY

dane copeland

First Edition

Printed in the U.S.

Published by college.u LLC

ISBN 979-8-9891439-0-0

Design and Layout by

Sandra Murray

contents

"...with resources and support,
the path to college could be navigated
with intentionality, keeping a student at
the center of their college journey
and reducing stress."

preface

If you judge a fish by its ability to climb a tree, it will live its whole life believing it is stupid. - Albert Einstein

You are going to college if you want to. You just don't know where yet." I say this almost every time I meet a student or parent. I believe this, and I think if you can believe this as well, a small piece of the anxiety that grips so many high school students and families might loosen and fall away. Each year, I hear students and parents with many college options continue to worry about what lies ahead. When I started college.u, I believed -- and still believe -- that with resources and support, the path to college can be navigated with intentionality, keeping a student at the center of their college journey and reducing stress. Working with students directly and providing free resources through the college.u website seemed the best way to reach more students and families and provide support to make college more accessible. Unfortunately, at times this still doesn't feel like enough.

With the increase of students successfully graduating from high school who want to pursue a college education, there is a need to rethink how to support students to ensure access and a successful college journey. I'm glad you're reading this book and are visiting college.u because it is for you -- to help you achieve your goals. It is not entirely a "how-to-apply-to-college" book because your college journey will be unique based on who you are. What makes you -- you might start with your interests, the classes you've taken in high school, or the activities you've engaged in -- whether living and breathing an activity 24-7, working after school, helping out your family -- and your community. How you spend your time now also might be what you will need in your college experience to allow you to flourish. These will differ from your friends, classmates, siblings, and neighbors. There are plenty of resources to help you get started, help you think about how you will approach your college journey, and hopefully rethink the myths and outdated information you may have heard.

I love education. There is so much to learn. If I could still be a full-time student, I would be. You may not feel the same way and have distinctly different reasons for attending college. Not surprising. Michael B. Horn and Bob Moesta asserted five reasons in their book, "Choosing College,"[1] providing a tidy framework. Whatever reason you are pursuing a higher education degree, be it a career, monetary security, intellectual curiosity, or the next step as you figure out what you want to be when you grow up, there are plenty of components you need to know when applying to college and things you can do to help you land where you want. Hopefully, this book will offer you the inspiration and some of the tools you will need for a successful college journey.

1 Horn, Michael B., and Bob Moesta. *Choosing College: How to Make Better Learning Decisions Throughout Your Life.* Wiley, 2019.

one

dream. search. apply.
simplifying the complex

After watching my two kids and their friends go through the college process and living in a community that highly values education, I recognized that the college search and application process, while complicated, does not have to be overwhelming. Instead, with the proper framework and guidance, students can easily have a college journey that supports their success with less stress. For parents, the college search process can feel like the culmination of parenting -- their child's final launch into adulthood. Nonetheless, even parents who recognize that their kids' college years will be filled with growth and change can be pulled into the anxiety of "getting into" college.

It reminded me of when my oldest was just about 18 months old, still scooting and crawling across the floor as a mode of getting from one room to another. No sign of the feet touching the floor, no noticeable interest in cruising around tables. Breaking out the latest "What to Expect" book to search for developmental milestones for children, I quickly found the note that said, "If your child isn't walking by 18 months, go see your pediatrician." I was immediately thrown into a state of a thousand questions and worries. Not surprisingly, what came to pass almost immediately after I scheduled an appointment with the doctor was my oldest taking those first, perfect, steps. My oldest had translated eighteen months of observing how others walked into his own seamless first steps. Conversely, my youngest began walking at nine months, propelled by a desire to catch up with everyone, and wore road rash and bumps as proudly as they embraced their tenuous mobility. In our hearts, we know each of our children is different, unique, and delightful, with their own sense of pacing. We're aware that they will develop on their own timeline, and yet, as parents, knowing we are not the initiators of the actual steps can make that part of parenting at arms' length and observation tortuous.

The milestones of graduating from high school, going to college, or choosing a different path are no different from a child's first steps: they are often internally driven and involve developmental readiness. Just like trying to determine which preschool would be the best fit, finding colleges that will be the best fit are part of the dreaming and searching. Dreaming in the college search is about broadening your scope to see the variety of colleges, programs, locations, and opportunities available as students begin their search. The crucial difference from when your child was two or three is that they are now ready to decide for themselves. Just as parents turn to "What to Expect" books, when their children are younger, getting up to speed on what has shifted in college admissions, is another way parents can learn "what to expect now" and see what's changed since they applied to college. Most students don't have a prior history of applying to college. It's all new stuff. They often carry years of familiarity with colleges that either family members attended, cheered for, or held as a totem of the best school. While these can be schools for students to begin exploring when starting their college search, it is essential not to fold the familiar into the idea of a "dream school." The mythical "dream school" -- that perfect, match-made-in-heaven school -- still circulates. However, it is no longer the sole, relevant factor in having a successful college search. I get it. It's hard to move away from an idea that may have percolated for 12 years, from the first alma mater t-shirt or basketball game.

My oldest was two weeks old, snuggled in a baby Bjorn watching their first blue and gold game. Not quite the start of building a college dream school, but it easy enough to be lured into the wish or wonder of it. After spending years walking across a campus quad to cheer the home team, it's so familiar and neighborly, and it would be hard for a student to stop thinking, "This is my campus." By removing the presumption that there is one single school for a student, families can help steer their teen towards a path of opportunity and encourage broadening their lens when looking at all the possible colleges available to them.

"College admission will get more complex before it simplifies, so focusing on the well-being of your child instead of the intricacies of the process is your best bet for success and your child's relationship with you and the world at large."

~ Forbes columnist Willard Dix

Simplifying the complex embraces putting a student's well-being at the center of their college journey and being proactive. Being proactive is a framework for the college journey that helps students and families move away from thinking that there is a singular "strategy" to "get into" college that has seeped into the college dialogue. "Strategic" carries both positive and negative connotations. Willard Dix's thinking in "Pros and Cons of Strategizing for College," Forbes Magazine,[1] still holds for how to strike the right balance for a successful process. Focusing on a student's pacing and college readiness is no different from when they were learning to walk. The wonderful and empowering quality they now possess is the emerging ability to express what they want and direct themselves where they want to go. Dreams allow for a more expansive way of thinking about what a student wants for their college experience, even if that means they are still determining what they want to major in or have everything precisely lined up. Finding colleges supporting exploration before declaring a major will be necessary for some students. Not all graduating high school students know what career or life path they ultimately want to pursue. Anchoring dreams in research and information will help establish expectations for students and families, whether about college costs, distance from home, curriculum structure, majors, or any other critical priority a student wants. Taking the time to search broadly, coupled with analysis and reflection on one's abilities and aspirations, allows for a stronger match between student and school and helps to define the equation for dream. search. apply.

---

1   Dix, Willard. *Pros and Cons of Strategizing for College.* Forbes Magazine.

rethinking the uncertainty in college admissions

I have been struck by the admission news trickling out in the past few years, particularly the stats from schools that offer only an Early Decision (ED or EDII – binding) or Regular Decision (RD – non-binding) application pathway. This news, coupled with Adam Grant's ideas of "rethinking what we know" in his latest book, "Think Again: The Power of Knowing What You Don't Know,"[2] resonated with me. What struck me wasn't the contrast between 1995 and now but the pace at which college admissions have changed in three short years. I've also been thinking about what information is offered to students and families to help them get up to speed and keep up with what to expect.

It would be easy to blame the media, with its continued focus on a select group of colleges often referred to as the elites, top schools, or "the highly rejective schools," [3] for providing a skewed view of college admissions, but there are plenty of experts providing students and families reliable information. Deciphering what it all means can still leave students, despite being surrounded by a vast pool of college options -- 4000+, still concerned that they won't get into college.

With this continued uncertainty in the nuances of college admissions, an overarching part of the equation is understanding the math of college admissions. Understanding the math runs from knowing that there are a finite set of seats at the table at even the large public universities, that the number of athletes that play on teams at a particular college may impact admissions, and that an increasingly large number of applicants are vying for those places.[4] Understanding that 98% of an accepted admitted class has a 3.75 GPA or higher (read 4.0 GPA or higher) also tells you that only 2% of admitted students have less than a 3.75 GPA. This command of the math can help students assess how likely they are to be admitted and how to balance the effort to apply against the chance of

2   Grant, Adam. Think Again: *The Power of Knowing What You Don't Know.* Penguin Publishing Group, 2021.

3   Akil Bello, *Twitter March 12, 2021*

4   Bauer, Jeremy. "Common App: Applications to highly selective colleges up by 25% in 2 years." Higher Ed Dive, 28 February 2022, Bauer, Jeremy. "Common App: Applications to highly selective colleges up by 25% in 2 years." Higher Ed Dive, 28 February 2022, Bauer, *Jeremy. "Common App: Applications to highly selective colleges up by 25% in 2 years." Higher Ed Dive, 28 February 2022,*

being accepted. Applying to more colleges equals more work and does not necessarily increase a student's chances of acceptance. Therefore it needs to be measured against the value of a student's time.

Paying attention to the big picture math can also help you rethink what you know about potential enrollment impacts, whether that takes the form of learning about the latest UC Berkeley News[5] limiting enrollment for this upcoming year, thinking through what fewer admit offers could mean and how that will roll forward across the other UCs and U.S. colleges, or learning when colleges like the University of Denver become an R1 school, Northeastern expands its campuses and learning pathways, or the University of Vermont adds an Early Decision application option.

The other side of the college admission equation is its unpredictable nature. This seems at odds with the predictability accompanying "math," but is tied to each college's mission. A familiar example is if a college needs a tuba player as part of its mission and enrollment goals. While it is difficult to know that, and even more challenging to become a tuba player overnight, if you do happen to be a tuba player, you may have an edge for admission to that school during that specific admission cycle. Unfortunately, students have little control over this part of the equation. While not a tidy example of the Heisenberg Uncertainty Principle, the pace of change and uncertainty over the last three-plus years has increased exponentially. Keeping track of all the changes can seem elusive. And even the Heisenberg theory,

"the uncertainty principle states that the more precisely the position of some particle is determined, the less precisely its momentum can be predicted from initial conditions, and vice versa."

regularly taught to college students, is less certain than previously understood. Common Interpretation of Heisenberg's Uncertainty Principle Is Proved False[6] -- another example of the power of "rethinking."

This means that a balanced list of colleges continues to be even more critical for students and underscores why students need to look beyond the

---

5   *UC Berkeley may be forced by court to cut 3,000 undergraduate seats, freeze enrollment*
6   Geoff, Brumfiel. *"Common Interpretation of Heisenberg's Uncertainty Principle Is Proved False."*
Scientific American, 2012

familiar school names attended by friends and family or schools with highly publicized sports programs. It also means incorporating multiple data sources, exploring a range of colleges and the costs to attend each school, and adopting a flexible application strategy, all of which will support building a best-fit college list. Sticking with what's important to you and how to meet your goals may require a step back to learn what is new in admissions and to rethink what you know when it's time to apply to college.

As you learn more about college admissions, take a breath and be open to rethinking how the shifts in this year's application cycle, e.g., waitlists, test-optional pathways, or expanded programs at colleges, impact students. Combining realistic expectations with aspirations and a strategy based on what you know has always been necessary, but that concept may need to be said out loud more often. Figuring out your personal math equation means distilling the numbers down from the approximately 4000+ colleges to the handful or so of schools, you will apply to and, ultimately, the one college you will attend.

....

big fish - little pond effect?
which pond will you swim in?

"How you feel about your abilities—your academic "self-concept"—in the context of your classroom shapes your willingness to tackle challenges and finish difficult tasks.
It's a crucial element in your motivation and confidence."

~ Malcolm Gladwell

The underlying sentiment of Malcolm Gladwell's "Big Fish- Little Pond Effect"[7] is the importance of determining what learning environment will support your success and which schools offer the educational setting to align with your goals. Understanding a college's learning environment and what type of "pond" it is should be as much of a guide as identifying curriculum, majors, campus culture, and opportunities

---

7 Gladwell, Malcolm. David and Goliath: *Underdogs, Misfits, and the Art of Battling Giants.* Little, Brown, 2015.

when researching and evaluating colleges. It is easy to assume that an elite or top-ranked school will provide the best educational opportunities for students. Gladwell's "big fish in a small pond" theory offers a framework for selecting a college that allows us to understand that the "best" school has more to do with how it meets a student's needs rather than how it ranks in a poll. Allowing students and families to consider the type of learning environment in their college search clarifies that there is no singular path in pursuing post-secondary education opportunities. Malcolm Gladwell introduced the term EICD Influence (Elite Institutional Cognitive Disorder) at his Google Talk in 2013,[8] which remains relevant to understanding why "relative position" may matter more than "absolute position" for a successful post-secondary experience. Not everyone will agree with Gladwell on this topic, but most will find value in a strong match between student and college.

"The phenomenon of relative deprivation applied to education is called—appropriately enough—the "Big Fish-Little Pond Effect." The more elite an educational institution is, the worse students feel about their own academic abilities."

~ Malcolm Gladwell,

David and Goliath: Underdogs, Misfits, and the Art of Battling Giants

While Gladwell bases his position partly on Mitchell Chang's work looking at students in STEM, the idea of relative position and its impacts can be applied more broadly. Including the concept of "learning or academic environment" in the college search can help students build a college list that offers opportunities, challenges, and balance. Focusing on the highly selective schools that gain regular media attention and reading articles about the one or two students accepted into every Ivy League school is practically a rite of spring.[9] This pond will be a comfortable

8   Malcolm, Gladwell. *Why Did I say "Yes" to Speak Here.*
9   "Absolutely Shocked': California Teen Accepted To 5 Ivy League Schools And Stanford." APRIL 11, 2021

environment for some students who thrive on challenge and rigor, but consider Ronald Nelson's story.[10] Nelson was admitted into every Ivy League and other highly selective schools but chose to attend the University of Alabama. Nelson looked at factors beyond "brand name." By selecting the Honors College at the University of Alabama, he found the school that was the best fit for him. Nelson created opportunities for himself and mitigated the cost factor of his education, graduating virtually debt-free. Regardless of which school a student ultimately attends, another critical piece of the equation is what a student can do while there. Selecting a school that will allow a student to take advantage of internships, research, advanced classes, community work, honors programs, or other opportunities will be a more rewarding experience. It can provide a foundation for graduate study or career opportunities.

As students begin their high school and college journeys, identifying the best educational environment, coupled with self-assessment and self-reflection, is vital to the college search. Determining a student's abilities, strengths, and college readiness will help answer the "big fish in a small pond" or "small fish in a big pond" question. Finding the right academic environment rather than simply choosing a "brand name" school can make all the difference for students today when weighing out college choices and supporting their education success.

....

building your foundation for college success

Whether you are considering applying to a highly selective school or not, there are advantages to having a strong foundation of core academic courses in high school. Considering course load and course selection in tandem with college requirements is ideal, but having a completed college list may not align with your timing for choosing your high school courses, especially as a first-year student. The questions of "How many years do I need in a particular academic area to be a competitive applicant?", "How can I strike the right balance to have more

---

10 Title:Ronald Nelson Turned Down Every Ivy League School for University of Alabama Website title:Business Insider

rigor but not be overwhelmed?" and the caveat, "What if I struggle with a particular subject?" are often at the top of the list for students and families when choosing classes in high school.

While there is no one answer for everyone, there are a few guideposts to consider when determining an appropriate robust academic foundation for you. The potential benefits of building such a framework and understanding the recommended and required courses colleges want to see in applicants' transcripts will keep your options open and help you think about building a solid academic foundation in high school. Taking a fourth year of math or three to four years of a language, even if these are not areas of strength, can positively impact applying to schools with low acceptance rates and managing college costs.

If you're interested in applying to a Western Interstate Commission for Higher Education (WICHE), aka WUE [11] school, which offers reduced tuition to residents in the Western states, know that there may be other requirements to qualify for reduced tuition. Recognizing if a WUE school, or any other school for that matter, requires applicants to have four years of math or achieve a specific standardized test score is an essential piece of the puzzle when applying to a college. While some high schools build their graduation requirements toward college application standards, not all do. While many colleges specify a minimum of two years of language, highly selective colleges will look for more rigor in your course load and class selection. Opting for depth rather than the minimum in an academic area is one way to demonstrate your ability to master a subject and the workload associated with it. This doesn't mean you need to load up on courses that will lead to an uphill battle. Striking the right balance should guide your decisions. As you move into senior year, you want to continue to lean into the right balance of challenges and not take your foot off the pedal. For many students, the 1st semester of senior year can be an opportunity to demonstrate academic strength that could bolster how a college reviews a student. Discerning what a particular college is looking for is part of the puzzle of whether a school matches you and where it falls on your balanced college list. While many colleges specify both recommended and required preferences that they are looking for in applicants, the word "recommended" at highly selective schools and the Ivies can translate to required."

---

11 Save On College Tuition | Western Undergraduate Exchange (WUE)

> So what can you do if you are not strong in a specific subject area like languages or math but are still interested in attending a school that will provide educational opportunities and rigor?

- Take the time to assess your interests and strengths to determine whether you genuinely align with colleges and their programs in a way that will lead to your success.

- Confirm the admission requirements before you commit to putting a college on your list to ensure it is a fit.

- Consider your educational options for taking a course that will be challenging, including online courses, community college courses, or incorporating support, such as Khan Academy, working with your teacher, finding a peer tutor, or hiring a professional tutor.

- Create a balanced college list with schools where you will thrive.

It is also reasonable to assume that the strong candidates in the applicant pool applying to highly selective schools have exceeded the requirements. The corollary to this is that hundreds of other schools offer rigorous, engaging academics that lead to success without enormous applicant pools and stringent requirements for acceptance.

Understanding the requirements for graduating from high school and applying to college extends beyond knowing how many years of math and languages to take and should also include a strong familiarity with a college's philosophy, curriculum, and mission. While each college's website should list this information on the admission page, the CollegeData.com[12] website is another great resource to learn about requirements and what colleges want. Building the most robust academic foundation possible for you is one piece of the puzzle in the college process. Whether in high school or college, your success will be defined by you. Knowing your strengths, abilities, and interests as you look through a 20-20 lens to begin your college search will help determine the right fit for you.

....

---

12 College Database Find the Best Colleges in US | CollegeData,

are you on the path to college?

P ursuing interests and goals by choosing classes or extracurricular activities you love can lead to rich opportunities. To formulate a balanced, future-oriented schedule, students should strive to pursue their interests and branch out of their comfort zone. In his article, Plan Ahead To Be College Eligible, Forbes contributor Willard Dix[13] captured the importance of considering what is foundational for attending college when evaluating which high school courses to take. He wrote: Many students planning for college look at a school's "minimum requirements for admission and think all they have to do is fulfill them to be admissible. Technically, that's true, but only technically. Simply meeting those minimums only gets you to the gate, not even close to the finish line. Even if you're considering attending your state institution, it's a mistake to assume you can slip in by completing the bare minimum for admission. What students and families may not realize is that the requirements for graduating from high school can be significantly different than what colleges require or "recommend."

For years, the narrative that "colleges don't look at freshman grades" has circulated in high schools and parent circles. This may be true for some universities (e.g., the UC system), as those universities focus on the 10th and 11th grades combined. However, the University of Chicago[14] released a study indicating that freshman grades matter. In short, the study found that grades in the 9th grade are strong predictors of high school success

---

Crucial questions to ask when formulating a schedule:

- What classes should you take if you struggle with a specific subject?
- Why do four years of math make a difference?
- Will you need to take three years of a foreign language?
- Should you double up in a subject area? It's also time to dispel the myth that freshman grades and courses don't matter.

---

13   Dix, Willard. "Plan Ahead To Be College Eligible."
14 Easton, John Q., et al. "The Predictive Power of Ninth-Grade GPA." 2017,

and college enrollment. Further, as Ashley Dobson stated in her NACAC Admitted blog, "A successful freshman year smooths the way for future success in high school and after." Students and parents should pay attention to the value of starting strong. Further, first-year students can choose classes that focus on maximizing strengths and balancing academics and interests outside the classroom.

"Let us make our future now,
and let us make our dreams tomorrow's reality."

-Malala Yousafzai

While the UC schools look closely at 10th and 11th grades and a holistic approach to assess which students get through the door, many colleges focus on first-year grades to see overall trends, the rigor of the courses a student has taken, and student interest. (Of course, students can and will still use their first year of high school to adjust to new course demands and to learn to negotiate the various hiccups that come with starting high school). While this new study indicates that freshman grades may strongly predict college success, students and families should not feel disheartened that the need to achieve now starts even earlier. Whether a student smoothly transitions into high school or is just developing the skills to succeed, the 9th-grade year provides valuable information to assess what is needed to support those learning outcomes. Choosing courses that engage and support student strengths in high school may be part of the equation that leads to success. There will always be bumps along the road, and learning early how to respond to challenges can provide a valuable lesson for students moving forward.

> **?** To further explore how small choices in high school have more significant implications, include these questions as part of your college search.
>
> - When do you need to start thinking about the college search and application process?
> - How does the college search and application timeline fit into your schedule?
> - When is the best time to start test prep?

It helps to have a roadmap. Knowing what to expect and what you must accomplish makes planning your academic future a more manageable, comfortable, and rewarding experience.

....

the college search timeline:
where is that tidy roadmap?

E very application season presents an opportunity to reevaluate the college search and application timeline and decide how to craft a plan to best support individual students. One consistent, counterintuitive message is that students should start their college essays in the fall. This timing works for many students, but for students not in a college-going culture or those with a lot on their plates, beginning in the fall might shortchange them of the valuable time the essay requires. Deadlines can create focus, but a key priority is ensuring that there will be enough time for essay ideas to percolate, have an authentic voice, and be polished before submitting. For other students, too much time is unhelpful and can create stress. So, as much as an overall timeline provides guideposts to high school students in general, ultimately, the college process works best when tailored to each student. One of the most salient and positive messages comes from the Berkeley Carroll School[15] website in New York:

> The reality is this: for this process to go well, it has to correspond to adolescent development and certain fixed benchmarks along the high school trajectory. Experience clearly shows that starting too early results in a process focused on the wrong ideas: "How do I get in?" becomes more important than "What am I looking for?" because this last question cannot yet be adequately tackled, regardless of how smart, mature, or high-achieving a student might be. - Berkeley Carroll School

I love the clarity in this. My role as a college counselor is to help keep the focus on "What am I looking for?" Remaining student-centered may involve nudging students to think broadly or holding the reins in a bit. Honoring each student's individuality facilitates a successful and manageable process and is a value integral to my work.

---

15   Berkeley Carroll School

admission transparency
and what you can control

"Grades and test scores used to be enough to get you in,"...
"Now, grades and test scores are just enough to
get you ready for further consideration."
- Jill Madenberg[16]

W hile books like "The Chosen"[17] and "The Price of Admission"[18] can lead students and families to think that admission is all about legacy, money, and "who you know," students have many opportunities to take control of their admission outcome and should not be dissuaded from driving their college search and application process. Admission rates are indeed dropping for some schools, but it's not all bad news, and it's difficult to point to one contributing factor. Jeff Selingo's "What Vanderbilt, Northwestern and other elite colleges don't say about acceptance rates"[19] article calls for colleges to be more transparent in the admissions process. Still, until that happens, there is much that a student can do to ensure a successful college search experience. Self-assessment of strengths and interests, research, investing in and using reliable resources, establishing realistic expectations, and building the necessary time are all critical factors in creating a successful college search experience.

These are all things within a student's control and completely achievable. With good planning, seeing the road ahead, and focusing on schools that match their strengths and goals, students can create their success.

---

16 Jeffrey Selingo. *"Perspective | What Vanderbilt, Northwestern and other elite colleges don't say about acceptance rates."* The Washington Post, 7 October 2017.

17 Karabel, Jerome, The Chosen: The Hidden History of Admission and Exclusion at Harvard, Yale, and Princeton, Houghton Mifflin, 2005

18 Golden, Daniel. The Price of Admission (Updated Edition): How America's Ruling Class Buys Its Way Into Elite Colleges--and Who Gets Left Outside the Gates. Crown, 2007.

19 Jeffrey, Selingo. *"What Vanderbilt, Northwestern and other elite colleges don't say about acceptance rates."* The Washington Post, October 7, 2017

TIP ONE: Build a college list that aligns with your strengths and interests.

TIP TWO: Research, research, research. Have the right tools & resources.

TIP THREE: Make a test plan that allows you enough time to prepare and optimize your abilities. Assess whether testing makes sense for you and if you should include test-optional schools on your college list.

TIP FOUR: Develop a timeline that works for you. The college search and application process takes time. Consider your schedule and time commitments to build enough time to accomplish tasks and meet deadlines.

TIP FIVE: Assess what kind of support you need to manage all aspects of your college search. Having the right tools and resources often includes someone with expertise to help you answer questions you don't even know to ask and assist in developing a successful strategy and plan.

big/little junior year and tips to find your balance

I*t's not a secret:* Junior year is no different from any other school year - you want to do your best. Doing that will be individualized, specific, and based on your strengths and interests and no one else's. So, why is there so much talk and emphasis about the junior year, and how busy is it? First, you are officially an upperclassman and may now take classes specific to your interests beyond graduation requirements. This is also when deepening or broadening your academic experience (by taking honors or AP classes, joining clubs, extending your interests outside of school, etc.) often takes place, which may require additional time. That can mean more to juggle.

You probably have also heard "Junior year matters" and 'Junior year is so hard." In one sense, each year you progress in high school will be a little more challenging than the year before.

That means assessing how many challenging courses you can handle so that you're not drowning in homework or, conversely, coasting through easy classes and missing opportunities to excel. A good goal for junior year is to aim for your sweet spot. Recognizing what you love and can handle both in and out of school is something you can work on now and a skill that you can apply to all aspects of your life. The bonus? Working on balance now will help you once you're in college. Junior year is also an academic year when colleges look at your class choices and how well you do in them. Colleges will be looking at the rigor in your courses and whether your grades are "trending up," which means demonstrating mastery and improvement throughout high school. At times it may feel like colleges will be sizing you up. Looking at what classes you take and how you do is part of how colleges determine if you will be successful.

Colleges want you to succeed and be able to handle the workload. Grades are one indicator of how a student will do as a college student, but college applicants are not evaluated solely on one data point, so approaching junior year with a positive attitude and embracing the idea of doing your best is part of the healthy equation of being an upperclassman.

Even though it may feel like the spotlight is on you during junior year, you can turn your spotlight on finding colleges where you will be successful. The college search is a two-way street. Carving out time to research schools during junior year is one way to set a manageable pace, so you will know what options are possible. The college journey is not a race, and just like planning an adventure or trip requires time and thought, you want to allocate time for your college search so it has a natural place in your life and doesn't overtake and drive every conversation and activity.

TIP ONE: Focus on your goals and your game plan and do things in a way that works best for you. Play your game, and try not to pay attention to what everyone else is doing.

TIP TWO: Strike a healthy balance that will include enough sleep, good food, exercise, and time with friends and family.

TIP THREE: Get a calendar and use it. I'll say it again: Get a calendar and use it. Do you like visual reminders? Get a whiteboard and hang it somewhere where you can see it daily. Pick a day to add events and deadlines for the upcoming week. Set your smartphone reminders or use an app to help you meet your deadlines.

TIP FOUR: Strike the right balance in your class load and find your sweet spot. Make a list of all of your classes and figure out which ones will need more time and which will be easier. Knowing how much time you will need in a week to study in addition to your other commitments and sleeping (8-10 hrs./ night) will help you see if you are achieving balance and if you need to make tweaks.

TIP FIVE: Develop self-assessment skills for knowing what is the right balance for you in and out of school.

TIP SIX: While the junior year will be busy, staying organized and focused on what's in front of you, being engaged in your classes, and pursuing activities you love will help you manage the right mix of challenges and fun

TIP SEVEN: Build in the time you need to think about what you want in your college experience. Determine what resources are available to identify priorities, goals, and strengths. Make a plan. That may include time to visit colleges to learn about the differences between private and public schools, urban, rural, and suburban settings, liberal arts and research universities, and the scale of small, medium, and large schools.

balance your college search with time

The stories of students unnecessarily applying to 20-plus colleges or submitting and facing deferral to only one Early Decision school are not urban myths but scenarios that can be avoided. Knowing when to begin to familiarize yourself with the college search and application landscape ensures adequate time to identify the qualities you would like in a college you want to attend. Starting college research, mapping out test preparation, visiting schools, and gathering materials for your applications takes time and organization. The difference between a positive and balanced college search and a stressful one often comes down to "pay now or pay later." Putting in the time upfront doesn't mean expanding the timeline but rather avoiding panic, poor timing, and late-night decisions later on.

The college essay, while daunting for some, is no different. Careful planning will allow you the space to write authentically and distinguish yourself.

Not everyone has access to a college counselor or essay coach, but there are plenty of sources to help guide you. Here are a few favorite books. Look for more on the books pages (pp. 141-143) and on the college.u website.

- Write Your Own Way[1]

- Escape Essay Hell[2]

- College Essay Essentials[3]

- On Writing the College Essay[4]

- Dartmouth General Study Tips

- The Most Productive Way to Schedule your Day

1 Toor, Rachel. *Write Your Way In: Crafting an Unforgettable College Admissions Essay.* University of Chicago Press, 2017

2 Robinson, Janine. *Escape Essay Hell! A Step-By-Step Guide to Writing Narrative College Application Essays.* CreateSpace Independent Publishing Platform, 2013.

3 Sawyer, Ethan. *College Essay Essentials: A Step-By-Step Guide to Writing a Successful College Admission Essay.* Sourcebooks, Incorporated, 2016

4 Bauld, Harry. *On Writing the College Application Essay, 25th Anniversary Edition: The Key to Acceptance at the College of Your Choice.* HarperCollins, 2012

Building in enough time to brainstorm, draft, and edit will support all different writing styles, from the deadline-driven to the multi-drafters. College essays have taken on a life of their own, with websites, books, and experts wholly devoted to how to master the essay. In addition to mapping out a timeline, there are plenty of resources for students that address key topics: where to start, topics to avoid, and why parent support is best only when requested (and then only for gentle proofing). What is vital to a successful essay is helping students find their voice, their story, and their words and gaining an understanding of where they fit in the context of seniors applying to college throughout the country and abroad. The anticipation and excitement of going to college can be critical motivators. Creating a timeline that incorporates enough time, the right tools, resources, and guidance will support this positive energy and lead to a more successful experience.

....

tackling tough tasks

"If it's your job to eat a frog, it's best to do it first thing in the morning. And if it's your job to eat two frogs, it's best to eat the biggest one first." ~ Mark Twain

While the first year of high school often entails acclimating to the new pace and demands of each class, sophomore year (or any year for that matter) is an opportunity to refine what has been learned and to create routines, develop skills, and add tools to help master what a student wants to accomplish. Learning how to tackle tough tasks early in high school can provide the scaffolding you'll want for your college years and beyond.

As a high school student, you may feel like returning to school is a bit of a kick to the head - thunk. Homework, weekly readings, and possibly an online class all take dedicated time and require assessing how you plan, organize and spend your days. The beginning of the school year or new semester is the perfect time for a fresh take on how to approach the months ahead and how to use your time in a way that works for you.

It's also an opportunity to develop study habits that will carry you from the built-in structure of high school to the self-driven college experience that requires a higher degree of ownership for studying. A few simple steps - finding the right place to study, implementing a system tracking assignments and deadlines, and creating time to study- will have a maximum positive impact. Many high school students utilize planner guides to manage priorities such as completing assignments, class projects, and preparing for tests. In addition, identifying priorities can help eliminate final cram sessions and the dreaded all-nighter and lead to sustained success.

Building strong study habits early is something high school students can benefit from before starting college. Implementing new habits can be as simple as taking a cue from Brad Stulberg's idea of shifting your mindset from thinking you need to create a big "change" to "adapting" and developing a routine.[20] If you follow college.u on Instagram or Twitter, you'll see that Stulberg's ideas on balance and working smarter fascinate me because they have such universal applications. Dr. Elizabeth Cohen Hamblet is another expert with invaluable advice on students and college and offers tools, "How-Tos," and insights about transitioning from high school to college. While Dr. Hamblet's book, "From High School to

Questions and resources to help you assess what you may need to make a shift in your work habits.

- Start with taking the Todoist Quiz to find out what productivity method will work best for you.

- Are you a visual person and prefer a whiteboard or planner to write tasks down?

- Do you like reminders that can be programmed into your phone, calendar, or computer?

- Would using an app that connects to something fun or meaningful be an additional perk or incentive to commit to a new strategy to organize your time?

20   Brad, Stulberg. *"The Truth About Routines."* Outside, 2020

College,"[21] is aimed at neurodiverse students, many of her suggestions on successfully managing a college workload can be applied to all students.

"Eating the Frog" is one approach that can transform the way you think about managing your time in a way that can diminish stress. For some students, it may be hard to shift to doing the most challenging items first, but it is not impossible. For those looking for techniques, tools, and tips, there are plenty, and the method is one to add to your toolkit.

Maximizing your time is not about subscribing to a philosophy where "productivity equals good." Instead, it's about valuing your time and goals in a way that allows you to put your energies toward the things most important to you and ensure you complete your required tasks.

....

Tools and RESOURCES to help with the intersection between managing time and your college search.

- www.stickk.com
- www.forestapp.cc
- www.notion.so
- www.us.livescribe.com
- www.remarkable.com
- 15 Best Journals & Planners for 2023: Our Readers' Favorites, Additude Magazine: www.additudemag.com/best-journals-planners-adhd-time-management/
- Dartmouth General Study Tips: www.students.dartmouth.edu/academic-skills/learning-resources/studying-tips
- The Most Productive Way to Schedule your Day: www.online-grad.syracuse.edu/blog/productivity/

---

21   Hamblet, Elizabeth C. *From High School to College: Steps to Success for Students with Disabilities.* Council for Exceptional Children, 2017

college.u
FRESHMAN CHECKLIST

2. Develop Healthy Routines

1. Put Tools in Place to Stay Organized

3. Create a Homework Routine

4. Sign up for Activities

5. Get to Know Your Teachers

7. Plan for Summer

6. Develop a New or Existing Skill

8. Build a Test Plan

9. Look for Classes Beyond Next Year

10. Congratulations - You Did It!

"If you had started doing anything

two weeks ago,

by today you would have

been two weeks better at it."

~ John Mayer

two

EXPLORING COLLEGES

building a great college list

Every student's college list needs to be as idiosyncratic as they are. Schools that are familiar because they are close to home or because Uncle George or a family friend attended will seem like easy options. Don't cross them off the list as you are getting started, they might lead to a school you should consider, but don't give them a gold star until you have done some deep research. Brand-name schools are tempting to put on a college list, but they may not necessarily translate into a good fit. While these may be good places to start, casting a small net may stifle students as they begin to align what they want in a school with their eligibility for admission.

Above all else, time is critical in building a successful list. Creating space to explore and identify a student's strengths, interests, and future aspirations allows a student to pinpoint colleges that will support them and enrich their college experience.

There are over 4000 schools to consider; why limit yourself when building your college list? At the core of building a balanced list, students must identify the key qualities essential to supporting their goals and success. Prioritizing what is important to you will lead to a college list that includes qualities that you want and, equally important, that you don't want.

- Do you thrive in small group discussions and face-to-face interactions with teachers? Look for schools that offer a small classroom environment with professors teaching first- and second-year courses. Check if professors or graduate students are teaching lower-division courses when looking at the student-teacher ratio. Schools that only allow upper-level students to access the small classroom experience may not be for you.

- Are you considering a larger campus to take advantage of a wide range of courses and activities but worry that you might get lost? Think about how to make a campus smaller by finding a niche, like a Learning Community, Honors College, or Residential Program.

- Consider schools that will offer flexibility in your academic path.

- Can you cross-enroll between colleges or programs? Investigating ways to expand your college experience through cross-enrollment or college exchange programs is just one avenue to explore before you finalize your college list.

- How easy is it to change majors or transfer colleges? You may enter college thinking you want to major in one area, but as you take courses, you may discover majors and programs more compelling that you hadn't considered before.

These are just some of the questions you can use when developing your college criteria. Once you start researching schools, looking at academics, curriculum, school size, culture, athletics, activities, location, and where to find your favorite foods, building a list of solid options should come into focus for you. Ultimately, there will be trade-offs as the list is refined, but casting a wide net will capture more options and opportunities and improve your chances of finding schools that match.

Looking beyond the familiar colleges, "media favorite" ranking lists, or colleges can feel like embarking on uncharted territory. With 4000 +

colleges to winnow down, having a few tools that can help identify and prioritize college criteria and preferences will clarify how to direct your college search.

College Criteria and Preferences: Corsava is one of my favorite resources that can be used by students, parents, and counselors. Unlike other college match tools to help students identify colleges that align with a student's criteria for building their college list, Corsava allows students to go deeper beyond the size of the school, location, etc.

Corsava is organized by Academics, Campus Culture, College, Educational Culture, Extracurricular Activities, Residential Life, and Student Resources, and offers a great starting point for learning about preferences and priorities. Corsava allows for a low-pressure, introductory assessment of what a student wants. Corsava can be used in a face-to-face or virtually, providing multiple options for students, families, and counselors to discover what is important to them. Students often don't realize the many possibilities for majors, extracurricular activities, college culture, and location. Corsava, coupled with discussions with a college counselor, school counselor, or parent, can be an excellent first step in assessing interests. The information extracted from this process can help students look for colleges that align with their interests and build college lists geared toward "fit." With the launch of the Corsava Student website, students now have another tool for their college search toolkit, and identifying key preferences just got easier.

The College Smell Test (College Visits): It's not hard to believe that once a student has identified the essentials for their college experience, the details about college culture, location, and even food will be equally significant to determining a solid fit. Not every student will visit before they apply, but they should visit before they commit to a school.

··

college fit goes beyond size and location

W hen looking for the perfect hiking boots, heels, or basketball shoes, you would never consider buying a pair that is too snug, too loose in the heel, or impossible to walk in for more than a few hours. Determining college size and fit is, in many ways, no different and involves understanding more than the location of the school and the number of students on campus. Discovering the academic landscape, type of curriculum offered (and delivered), and available resources can help determine if a school has the educational environment you seek. The mix of combinations can range from schools that champion core foundation requirements or emphasize inter-departmental and independent majors. Knowing if a college hosts

---

These questions are a good jumping-off point to help you start your deep-dive:

- What is the Academic Landscape? Primarily Tech? Liberal Arts? Comprehensive University? Tech w/ Liberal Arts College?

- What is the Curriculum offered? Open? Structured? Hybrid?

- How are students admitted into programs? Admission to Major (Direct admit)? Earn your way into a major?

- What is the first-year experience? Can students take classes in their major? Are students limited to General Education and pre-requisite classes? Are there required common courses for all incoming first-year students?

- What is the Class Size for your average class and required courses?

- Is there a capped class size for English/Math/Science and major? What is the class size range at a larger university - is it 40 or 400 students? Are labs limited to a set number of students?

- What is the retention rate? Find out the return rate of first-year students for each college. Are there specific majors with a reputation for losing students to other related majors?

- What is the graduation rate? Can you complete your undergraduate work in four years, or will it require more time, and if so, why?

- Are there accelerated programs that combine completing an undergraduate degree and a master's, e.g., (3-2 or 4+1) offered?

a library lending program, facilitates cross-enrollment between colleges within the university or between multiple universities, and has study-abroad programs primarily during the junior year or throughout the academic calendar can be the type of insight you need to determine if a college aligns with your educational goals. Identifying specifics of the educational environment may include looking at the support a college provides regarding academic advising, tutoring, first-gen programs, internships, and career placement. When starting your college search,

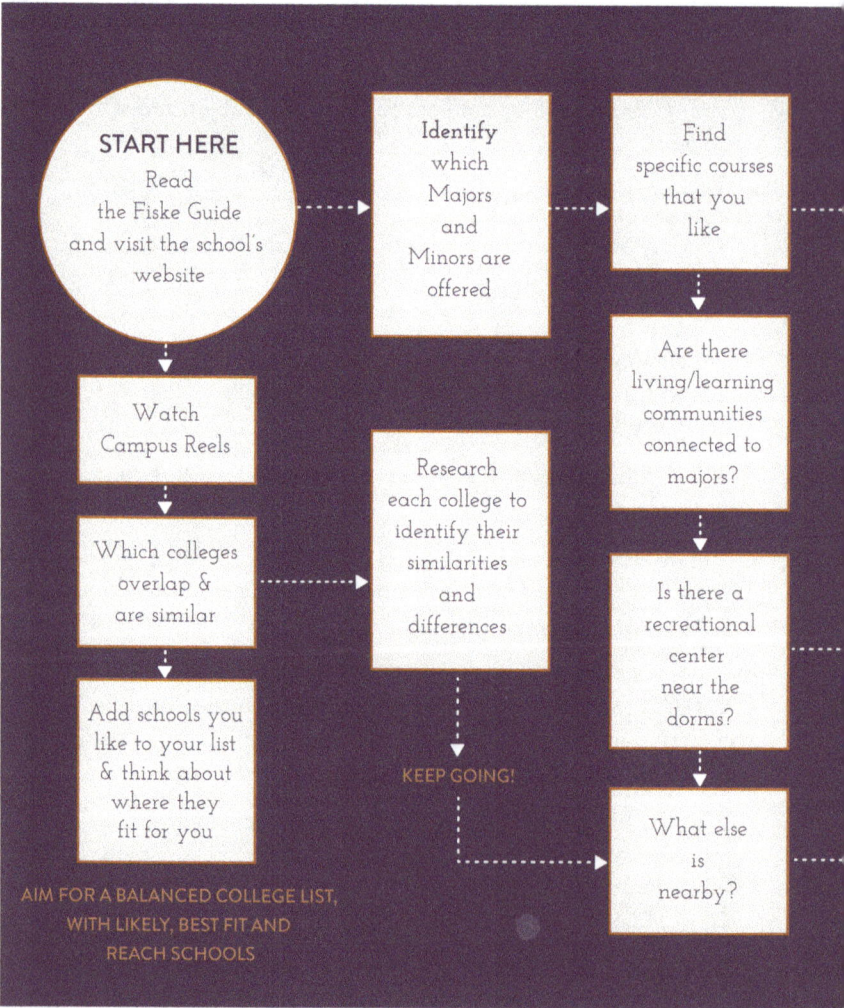

START HERE
Read the Fiske Guide and visit the school's website

Identify which Majors and Minors are offered

Find specific courses that you like

Watch Campus Reels

Research each college to identify their similarities and differences

Are there living/learning communities connected to majors?

Which colleges overlap & are similar

Is there a recreational center near the dorms?

Add schools you like to your list & think about where they fit for you

KEEP GOING!

What else is nearby?

AIM FOR A BALANCED COLLEGE LIST, WITH LIKELY, BEST FIT AND REACH SCHOOLS

take the time to look beyond location and size, and dive into a school's academic culture and mission so you can determine your perfect "fit."

How will you answer these questions? Dive into virtual information sessions, student chats, and virtual tours to answer these questions. Look for on-campus opportunities like department-specific events or programs where prospective students can shadow classes. Recognizing the differences and similarities between schools will help you identify colleges that will fit you.

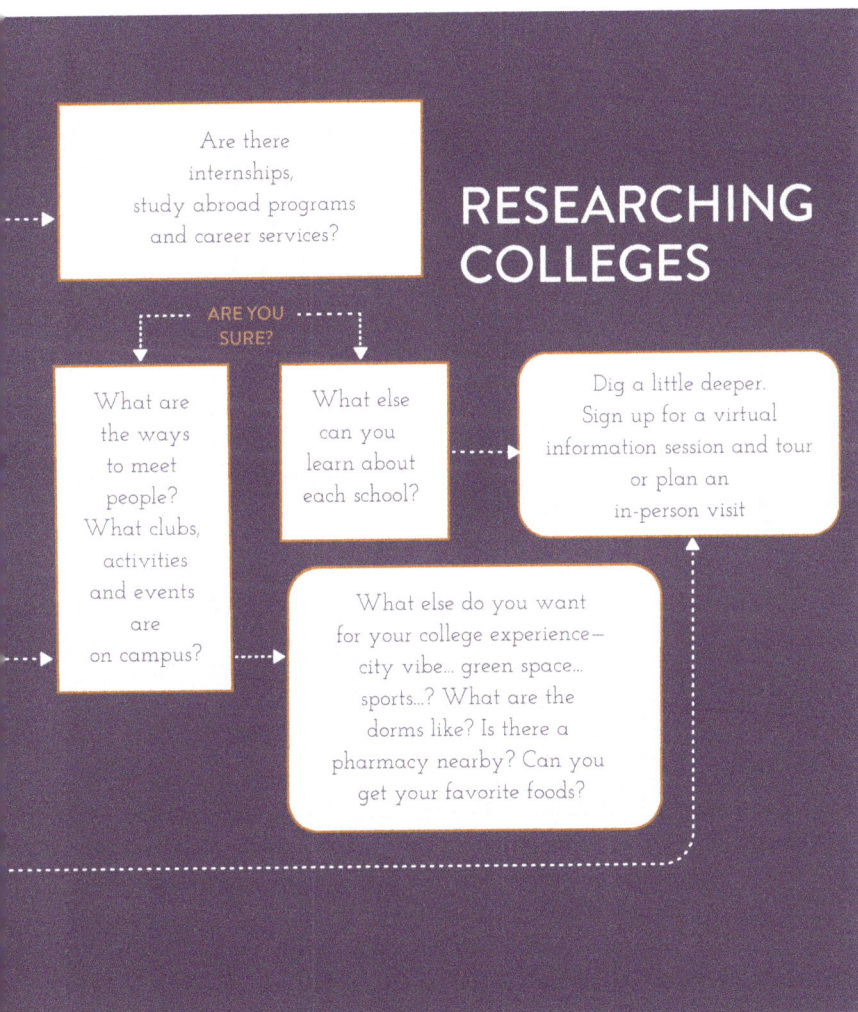

RESEARCHING COLLEGES

Are there internships, study abroad programs and career services?

ARE YOU SURE?

What are the ways to meet people? What clubs, activities and events are on campus?

What else can you learn about each school?

Dig a little deeper. Sign up for a virtual information session and tour or plan an in-person visit

What else do you want for your college experience— city vibe... green space... sports...? What are the dorms like? Is there a pharmacy nearby? Can you get your favorite foods?

- Fiske Guide to Colleges[1]

- Where You Go Is Not Who You'll Be: An Antidote to the College Admissions Mania, Frank Bruni [2]

- College Match: A Blueprint for Choosing the Best School for You [3]

- CollegeXpress [4]

- College Scorecard[5]

- Colleges That Change Lives[6]

- Higher Ed Data Stories[7] IPEDS[8]

1   Fiske, Edward. *Fiske Guide to Colleges 2023*. Sourcebooks, Incorporated, 2022.
2   Bruni, Frank. *Where You Go Is Not Who You'll Be: An Antidote to the College Admissions Mania*. Grand Central Publishing, 2016
3   Antonoff, Steven R. *College Match: A Blueprint for Choosing the Best School for You*. Steven R. Antonoff, 2019
4   CollegeXpress: Scholarships, College Search, Lists and Rankings,
5   College Scorecard | College Scorecard
6   Colleges That Change Lives – Changing Lives. One Student At A Time.
7   Boeckenstedt, Jon. Higher Ed Data Stories
8   "IPEDS " Integrated Postsecondary Education Data System NCES

march madness
and framing your college search

Could your college search begin as a March Madness Bracket sheet? For some students, this may be the perfect way to start building a college list. The key is doing ample research and knowing your colleges just like you know the difference between the @bigten and the @accmb. While you don't need to look at 64 schools to begin your college journey, look broadly at different types of schools to familiarize yourself with the characteristics, similarities, and differences between schools. Could you even start with schools participating in March Madness? Based on past March Madness years and the buzz around conference play each year, there definitely can be a range of schools to check out, from public universities like the University of Michigan, Georgia Tech, and Cal State Fullerton to private schools like Gonzaga, TCU or Villanova, or schools you weren't familiar with like Saint Peters.

Building a college list involves synchronizing your interests with what a college offers to form a balanced equation. One side of that equation is coming up with your list of priorities you want for your college experience, which can include the type and breadth of courses offered, retention rate, academic advising, professor-student ratio, flexibility in choosing a major, cost to attend, and even a great basketball team.

The other side of the "building your list equation" is sizing up what colleges look for in applicants and how they review students. What schools look for can vary widely and can include, for example, an emphasis on residency, specific interests, and talents, recommendations, the first generation to attend college, essay, or relation to alum.

Colleges don't solely rely on statistics like GPA and test scores, but GPA and high school rigor are parts of the holistic methodology colleges use to try and predict if students will succeed on campus. Colleges want to see their students succeed. Schools also want to learn about added qualities or interests that students would contribute to their campus. Sometimes that is readily apparent in what a student does outside of school and how that reflects a student's values or character.[1]

Matching up to a college is a two-way street. It is as much about what a student wants as part of their college experience- meeting future friends for life, internships, building career, alumni connections, or a particular type of academic curriculum - as it is about what a college wants.

If a school has a focus on social justice or community engagement and you have dreams of working in a lab or doing research, think about if this is the perfect place to try your hand at something new or if it makes better sense to focus on areas that highlight robust undergraduate research opportunities.

_____

1   Barnard, Brennan. "New Research Finds That Character Counts In College Admission." Forbes, 2020

> So how do you start to figure out if you're a match? Here are a few TIPS to add to what you're already doing:
>
> - TIP ONE: Read a college's Mission Statement.
>
> - TIP TWO: Start a list of what you want for your college experience.
>
> - TIP THREE: Track what each college has at their school - courses, clubs, study abroad, support services, etc. While you can use a college matching tool like College Scorecard or CollegeXpress, go to the source - each school's website to do your research.
>
> - TIP FOUR: Look beyond what majors are offered.
>
> - TIP FIVE: Look deep into majors to learn how courses are taught and structured over four years. See what activities are offered and highlighted.

While there are approximately 4000 + colleges to look at, the reality is that you're going to only sift through some of them. Defining what specific qualities you are looking for will help you sort through potential colleges and develop a reasonable research list. Be aware of the "name familiarity" influence. Brennan Barnard explains how "name familiarity" can influence students when choosing colleges to be on their list in his article, "The College Admission Blind Taste Test,"[2] and offers thoughts on reframing how to look for colleges. While it may be hard to avert your eyes from rankings or schools with name-brand recognition looking beyond the familiar can help students discover the multitude of colleges that will support their aspirations.

Here's a fun fact: schools seeded for March Madness can have an uptick in applications.[3] Whether you literally explore schools that have teams playing in March Madness or use the bracket structure to look broadly and then narrow down your list of schools to a balanced list, the essential part is to get to know schools well and have a realistic understanding of how well you and the school match. Having a balanced list of likely, best-fit, and reach schools will ensure that you turn the March madness into a college journey that helps you make your shot.

---

2 Barnard, Brennan. "The College Admission Blind Taste Test." Forbes, 2018

3 Glatter, Hayley. "The March Madness Application Bump." The Atlantic, 2017

finding your people. finding your pride.

College vibe, culture, and community are often at the top of the list of priorities once academics and majors have been identified when researching colleges. Where are the first places to look for clues to discover what a college culture is like? Will it be the offerings of clubs, activities, sports teams, or even community service as an extension of what was available in high school? Will it be something new? All of those aspects are excellent places to begin and will provide a great jumping-off point for another critical part of your search - the people involved in those activities. As a high school student, you may want a like-minded community at your college or be looking to expand your community. No matter what you are looking for, finding "your people" requires dedication to unearth who exactly comprises each community and is time well spent. Most likely, many people form the wide range of communities that contribute to a university environment, some based on academic interests, shared values, or even demographic origins.

Many colleges value and talk about building diverse communities and campus cultures, but diversity can live on a spectrum depending on

---

LGBTQIA questions to start with (be sure to create your own list of essential information as well).

- What are LGBTQIA groups on campus?
- Are there LGBTQIA academic groups?
- Are there LGBTQIA Support Groups?
- Are there faculty members that are part of LGBTQIA groups?
- Is there gender-neutral housing?
- What medical services do Health Services cover?
- Are fraternities and sororities diverse and inclusive?
- Is there a mission statement on the campus website that reflects the school's values?
- Is there training for faculty?
- What academic offerings are there?

For additional LGBTQIA resources, see pp. 156-160.

---

college location or commitment to programs and students. The first step is to see beyond college mailers and know what to look for on each college website. Once you have done your homework, stepping on campus and meeting with current students, professors, or alums will help paint a clearer picture. So how can students and families find out if a campus is inclusive, welcoming, emerging, or transitioning to embrace LGBTQIA students? What resources will be good indicators of where a university is on the spectrum, and what questions will help you find out? Each college website should provide information and clues.

> ✔ College vibe, culture, and community are often at the top of the list of priorities, so how can you learn more about each college?

- What academic offerings are there?

- You may want to sign up for the school paper if it is online to keep up with what is happening on campus.

- When visiting campuses, either before you apply or after you've been accepted, visit organizations and pick up materials that explain what resources and support are in place for students.

look under the hood

S UV, sedan, electric. Are you saving up for your first car, or can you remember the last time you purchased a car? How are you deciding which car will be best for you? Are you reading Consumer Reports, looking at the Kelly Blue Book values, or Edmunds? Have you talked to friends and family members about cars you were considering? Or you've been test-driving a handful of cars to determine if they have what you want. What are your top priorities - leg capacity, responsive steering, or gas mileage? And what tools are you using to assess the value of each? Finding the best-fit colleges is no different from looking for the right car

Using various resources (like @Clark2College[4]) is necessary to determine if a school meets your key priorities. When using websites, resources, and search tools, it is also critical to know the source and context of the data. For example, ranking lists often use criteria such as endowment size and peer review to develop a composite rank. While this may be interesting, it may not translate to student support, focus, or success. Rankings, popularity, and national reputation may contain some information that is good to know, but you'll want to look past the ranking numbers to understand what's being evaluated. Malcolm Gladwell's recent "Lord of the Rankings"[5] podcasts pull back the curtain about rankings and provide invaluable insights if you're starting your college journey. Just like considering car design or how fast a car goes from 0 to 60 mph when investing in a car, you want to look under the hood when starting your college search.

Take the time to learn the difference between programs at different schools, as no one size fits all. Smith, Colorado School of Mines, and 3-2 programs are excellent examples of how engineering programs can vary significantly. While engineering is offered at each school, how the degree is accomplished is unique and tied to their educational missions. If the size of the school is essential, look more closely at the numbers to learn how they define the campus community.

While many schools have a similar number of undergraduates, do those similar schools provide the same number of majors or focus on particular areas of study, such as a polytechnic or art school? Even when looking at what appears to be similar schools like large public universities, the range of what and how many majors are offered, and their focus can vary. Looking beyond reputation and ranking and digging into details is a step that will reveal if a school has what you want.

location, location, location

If you live in California or a place where you are tired of cold, humidity, or hot summers and want a taste of the West Coast, you may be thinking that California public universities are large, less expensive, and have robust offerings of majors. This is true for the most part, but each school has its distinct curriculum, focus, and mission. For example, while one

4   Clark, Rick. "Rick Clark (@Clark2College)." Twitter
5   Gladwell, Malcolm. Lord of the Rankings. no. Season 6, Episode 2, Revisionist History Podcast

- Does the major have a lockstep curriculum?

- Are there required courses that lead to declaring a major?

- Does the major have a direct admission or pathway to apply at the end of sophomore year?

- Instead of majors, is there an open curriculum where you design your academic focus?

- Do you take courses for your major one block at a time?

Take the time to learn the difference between programs at different schools, as no one size fits all. Smith, Colorado School of Mines, and 3-2 programs are excellent examples of how engineering programs can vary significantly. While engineering is offered at each school, how the degree is accomplished is unique and tied to their educational missions. If the size of the school is essential, look more closely at the numbers to learn how they define the campus community.

- Is the number of enrolled students composed primarily of undergraduates or a combination of undergraduate and graduate students?

- What do the demographics (gender makeup, out-of-state vs. in-state, etc.) tell you?

- Do students live on campus?

- Does the school primarily support commuter students, and if so, how does that impact the campus community and culture?

- Are activities like sporting events, concerts, or movie nights offered on weekends?

- Do students seek out the surrounding community for local events?

California school may offer majors in Economics, Communications, and Marketing, it may not provide a major in Business.

Suppose you're concerned about costs and looking for ROI (return on investment). In that case, look for hands-on experiences like internships, access to career or job fair opportunities, or alums networking to jumpstart job opportunities after graduation. While many schools offer internship opportunities, the range of how they are offered, whether they are optional, folded into the curriculum, or are a graduation requirement, can vary.

Finding out if a school provides internship opportunities, whether it is incumbent on the student to secure one, or if an internship is part of a senior capstone project or during a specific semester/quarter or summer are all aspects of the sleuthing students want to do when researching colleges.

What tools should you use when building your college list? Utilizing books and websites like College Scorecard is an excellent first step, and college.u has curated a host of resources for DIY students and families, but you'll also want to go to the source. Dive deep into each college's website. Explore majors offered, graduation requirements, clubs, athletics, and any other quality you want in your college experience. This will help you see if what a college offers align with your goals and provide insights into what each school values.

Purchasing a car takes time and is not something you pick up on the way home from work or order online, and building a college list is no different. Taking the time to look under the hood, whether exploring colleges or cars, is essential and something you will want to do before making your down payment.

....

make the college environment
support your neurodiverse excellence

"If we are to achieve a richer culture, rich in contrasting values, we must recognize the whole gamut of human potentialities, and so weave a less arbitrary social fabric, one in which each human gift will find a fitting place." -Margaret Mead

T homas Armstrong, in the article, "The New Field of Neurodiversity: Why 'Disabilities Are Essential to the Human Ecosystem'"[6] writes: "Success in life depends upon modifying your surrounding environment to fit the needs of your unique brain" which pivots the question facing neurodiverse students about attending college from "Can I," but "How To?" Diversity in the post-secondary environment enriches the learning experience for all students. Although having any health issue may seem like an obstacle for a student that wants to attend college, it is an obstacle that can be addressed, not a deterrent. Armstrong believes that cultural context helps to frame how we think of someone -- gifted or disabled. Armstrong asserts that context as perspective can help to reframe characteristics as strengths vs. flaws.

"Success in life is based on adapting one's brain to the needs or the surrounding environment."

- *Principle # 5, Thomas Armstrong*

"Success in life also depends on modifying your surrounding environment to fit the needs of your unique brain."

-*Principle #6, Thomas Armstrong*

Students' varying strengths, abilities, and interests can impact their educational experiences. Each student's unique qualities lend themselves to making a richer and more interesting college environment and creating academic and career success.[7] Yes, some colleges are looking for a particular "type" of student with a more narrowed academic focus, but even those colleges will build a more well-rounded community. Diversity of intelligence and abilities does not preclude a student from attending college.[8] What is essential during the college search is ensuring there is more than adequate support for student success at the colleges they are considering. For example, the SALT program at the University of Arizona[9] is often cited and regarded as taking the lead in offering student

---

6 Armstrong, Thomas. The Power of Neurodiversity: Unleashing the Advantages of Your Differently Wired Brain (published in Hardcover as Neurodiversity). Hachette Books, 2011
7 Pisana, Gary P. "Neurodiversity as a Competitive Advantage." Harvard Business Review, 2017
8 "The Learning Effectiveness Program | Student Affairs." DU Student Affairs
9 SALT Center: Welcome

support, but with research, students, and families will find several schools that have developed program support for neurodiverse students.

To ensure there are appropriate resources and support in place, assessing these areas will help:

- How does the school support neurodiverse students?
- Is it through the Disability Office, Academic Support Center, Wellness or Support Center?
- What support systems are in place on campus?
- Is there flexible or priority class scheduling? What are the specific academic support programs in place and who works with students?
- Do those services cost extra, or are services included with tuition or an additional student fee?
- Can you have a modified Test Scheduling?
- What Wellness and Health Services are available?

Is there a cap on the number of visits?

- What is the wait or scheduling time for appointments? Is there a drop-in option?
- Housing and Meal Service?
- What services will you need off-campus?
- Is there local transportation to those services and easily accessible from campus?

Once you've been admitted into a school, what steps must you take to ensure you have the proper support on campus?

- What documentation must you or your high school provide at the start of each school year, semester, or quarter?
- What advocacy skills will you use to ensure you have the support you need?
- How will you communicate what you need to your Academic Advisor, Professors, and Dorm R.A. - through forms, emails, or verbally, the Disability Center?

It is easy to think that attending college involves strictly adhering to rules and protocols that are set up for the general student body. What is often overlooked is that there may already be support systems in place for neurodiverse students or that students may need to advocate for what they specifically need to achieve success. Incorporating a

RESOURCES, ARTICLES AND VIDEOS

- College Disability Accommodations Information - Elizabeth C. Hamblet
- How Companies Are Increasing Neurodiversity in the Workplace[1]
- Don't Ignore Mental Health Services When Evaluating Colleges[2]
- ADA.gov: The Americans with Disabilities Act
- Bring Change to Mind - Let's Talk Mental Health
- Active Minds - Changing the conversation about mental health
- Wrightslaw Special Education Law and Advocacy
- "College Programs." CollegeAutismSpectrum.com
- "Postsecondary Education (College or University)." Autism Speaks
- Depression and Bipolar Support Alliance: DBSA
- NAMI: National Alliance on Mental Illness
- A Work in Progress: A Scholar's Story[3]
- Disability or Divergent Characteristic: Inside the Neurodiversity Movement[4]
- Meet Elyn Saks, J.D. P.H.D., Professor at USC, Board member of the Reintegration Project The Factors for Living a Productive Life - Youtube[5]

1   "How Companies Are Increasing Neurodiversity in the Workplace." Knowledge at Wharton, 2019
2   Wolf, Nancy L. "Evaluating Mental Health Support of a College." Road2College, 25 March 2022
3   "A Work in Progress: A Scholar's Story — The Center for Reintegration." The Center for Reintegration, 6 November 2019
4   Nyhan, Sean. "Disability or Divergent Characteristic: Inside the Neurodiversity Movement." NACA, Journal for College Admissions, 2018
5   Saks J.D., PhD., Elyn. The Factors for Living a Productive Life.

balance between Thomas Armstrong's assertions and Principles[10] can create an environment where students will thrive in college. Deciding where to go and knowing which colleges value neurodiversity requires time and research.

Review the Mission Statement, programs, curriculum, and majors. Ask questions. Visit. Don't limit yourself to just the website. Can't find an answer to a question? Send a follow-up email to admissions.

····························

blue light

W hen students and families are touring a campus, beyond discovering that tour guides are skilled at walking backward and may swing the tour by the student center to buy school swag, there will be that moment when the guide highlights the blue light and other safety features that each school provides. While this portion of the tour may be sandwiched between study abroad programs, the latest trending majors or new buildings on campus, campus safety is an area you don't want to overlook.

What safety means often goes beyond hitting a button on the blue light pole or the response time from campus security or police. Surveying a broader swath beyond the campus borders will help you determine if the school and the community[11] have the resources that support a safe environment and are located where your studies remain front and center

Learning about a school's location requires understanding more than the seasons, whether there is air-conditioning in the dorms, what and how a Jan-term between the 1st and 2nd-semester works, or how near or far from a major city the school is located. Understanding the safety parameters a school can (or cannot) enforce (which vary by state) may be something students and families had not considered but may want to now. Understanding what health care services, including student health insurance, are offered on and off campus should be factored in as the services provided varies from state to state.

---

10 Armstrong, PhD., Thomas. "Neurodiversity | Thomas Armstrong, Ph.D." American Institute for Learning and Human Development

11 Truong, Debbie. Winton, Richard. Watanabe, Teresa.
"How UC, CSU prepare for active shooters." Los Angeles Times, 15 February 2023

Discovering campus culture, policies, and values may take additional research to determine what unites the student community. Some colleges rally around their sports teams, the well-being of their students, local events on campus, social fraternities and sororities, academic clubs, or community engagement programs that support their local city as outlets for students to find their people. Just knowing the percentage of students joining campus social clubs, e.g., the number of clubs, living-learning communities, and ways a student can engage, whether at a large public university like Clemson University or a smaller school like Davidson College, can be a telling factor and help a student assess campus culture. Beyond visiting schools, simply picking up or subscribing to

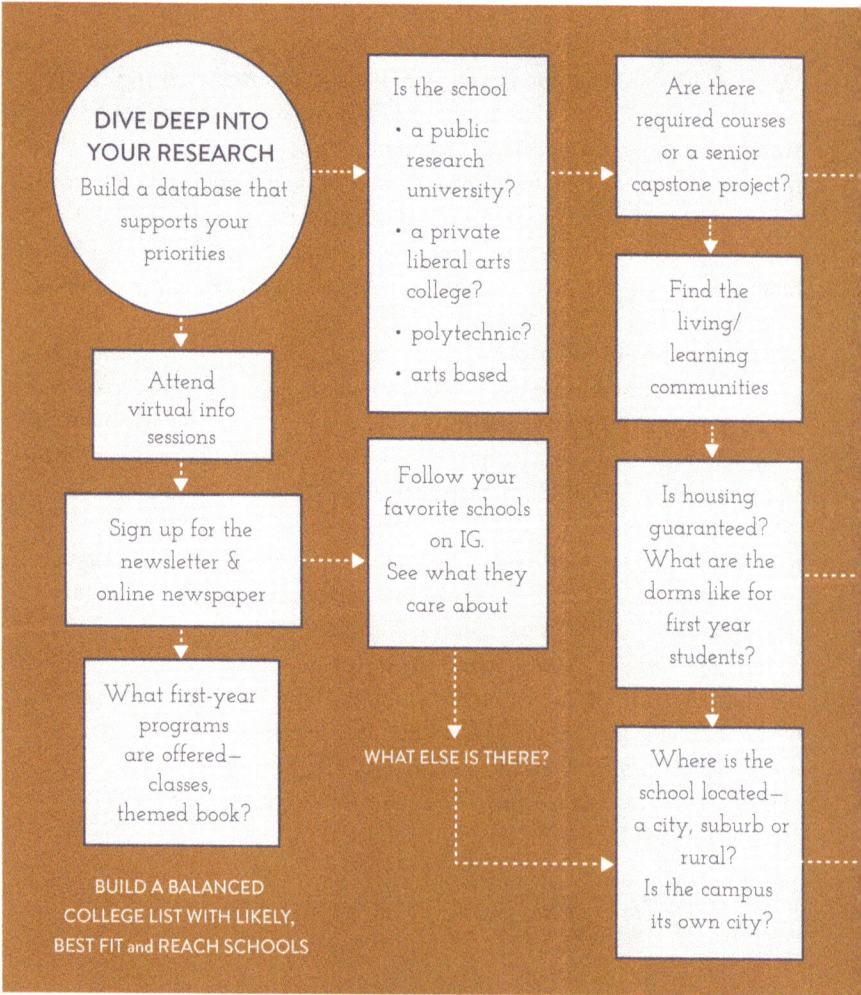

DIVE DEEP INTO YOUR RESEARCH
Build a database that supports your priorities

Attend virtual info sessions

Sign up for the newsletter & online newspaper

What first-year programs are offered— classes, themed book?

BUILD A BALANCED COLLEGE LIST WITH LIKELY, BEST FIT and REACH SCHOOLS

Is the school
• a public research university?
• a private liberal arts college?
• polytechnic?
• arts based

Follow your favorite schools on IG.
See what they care about

WHAT ELSE IS THERE?

Are there required courses or a senior capstone project?

Find the living/ learning communities

Is housing guaranteed? What are the dorms like for first year students?

Where is the school located— a city, suburb or rural?
Is the campus its own city?

the student-run newspaper can provide invaluable insight into what is happening on campus and what matters to current students. Discovering if a school is a fit goes beyond understanding statistics, and learning how schools value and ensure the safety of their students is an important aspect to explore. When I began writing this post weeks ago, it was before the unthinkable events at MSU that again put a fine point on safety in the college environment and what schools do to ensure a safe environment for learning. And while we can't shield ourselves from circumstances beyond our control, we can assert expectations and be intentional regarding where we want to be, and which schools will support our aspirations.

DEEP COLLEGE RESEARCH

Can you take courses in another country or cross-enroll with another school?
Find the countries and courses

DONT STOP HERE! - -
KEEP GOING

Are there 3+2 degrees that combine a B.A. with a M.A.?

What is the campus vibe— mellow, competitive, focused on team spirit?

Can you have access to professors through small classes or research?

Have you visited, demonstrated interest, attended a hosted event (virtual or local)?

What else do you want for your college experience?

know your onions:
be prepared for college visits

The beloved protagonist of Shrek once said that "ogres are like onions." Why, you might ask? "Onions have layers. Ogres have layers," is the explanation that Shrek gives us. While we're formulating our list of things that are like onions, why not add colleges? Colleges, like ogres and like onions, are complex and require more than a first glance to understand what's inside. That is where the college visits come in. Making intentional choices about which schools to visit, whether grouped by type of school, programs, or region of the country, will help focus the time on campuses and minimize the cost of separate visits. College visits can have a lasting impact on students and families as they begin to explore colleges, so developing explicit criteria for why to visit a school is an essential step in the college search.

Plan to see a range of schools. If you are unsure of what type of school you want to attend or if you already know the kind of program or school you are looking for, seeing a variety of colleges will allow you to compare schools apples to apples. A range of schools can encompass private, public, urban, rural, small, and large universities. It's one thing to know the enrollment size at a campus, but another to experience it first-hand. Keep in mind that if you are visiting during the summer, you are most likely not seeing full-time students and the campus in full swing.

Tips for maximizing your college visits:

- For every school you put on a list that you have heard of, try including one or two schools that you haven't heard of before. You increase the list of schools to explore beyond name recognition by doing that.

- Planning a trip to the Midwest area? Consider visiting Lake Forest College, Loyola University, DePaul University, Wheaton College, Illinois Institute of Technology, University of Illinois Chicago, and School of the Art Institute of Chicago in addition to Northwestern University and The University of Chicago.

- Want to check out other Midwest schools? The Liberal Arts Colleges comparison tool can help you sort through the differences between schools like Kenyon College and College of Wooster, located in Ohio and only one hour apart.

- How does a liberal arts college differ from a research university? What is a liberal arts college? The terms college and university are often thought of as offering the same educational opportunities, but actually can be entirely different. Identify which schools are liberal arts colleges or Colleges That Change Lives. Incorporating one or two visits will add dimension to your college visits and possibly your college list.

- Which campuses offer both research and liberal arts? Tufts, the University of Michigan, and Emory University are just a few examples of colleges that provide this type of educational environment.

- What are the advantages and disadvantages of attending curriculum-focused schools like Cal Tech, Georgia Tech, Cal Poly, or an art school like California Institute of the Arts and Rhode Island School of Design? You'll want to find out if there is flexibility in changing your major or focus.

- What are some of the differences between private and public universities? Is it just size? One common mistake is to assume public universities are less expensive to attend automatically. Before you go, check out what kind of financial aid is offered – merit- and need-based. While a public university may be larger, does it have a significant enough endowment in addition to state and federal funding to offer the kind of aid you need to attend?

- What kind of specialized programs and opportunities are offered? While some schools may have a national reputation or are known for something in particular, don't miss the chance to hear firsthand what a school values and explore other programs that aren't as apparent.

- Are there internships and research opportunities for undergraduates? The University of Chicago is happy to inform you that they have more research internships available than students. Do you consider travel an essential part of your college experience? Find out if the study abroad program has an additional cost. Wellesley College offers an excellent example of how the cost of studying abroad may be structured. With some schools, your tuition includes your semester abroad. Of course, make sure to read the fine print for any add-ons.

- What kinds of academic curriculums are offered? - Core, Block, or Individualized major? Can you double major or add a minor? Try to find out if doubling up on majors is the norm. For some students, that option will be the perfect solution to combining their interests, but not every student wants that type of rigor, so it's good to know the academic culture and expectations.

- Every student is unique—tailoring college visits to align with specific needs and goals will put you on the path to a meaningful college experience.

....

expanding and personalizing your college experience

Trying to determine your best-fit colleges requires knowledge about a variety of characteristics, including curriculum and the learning environment each college offers. Understanding class size, teacher-student ratio, and how courses are taught will provide insight into the range of learning environments colleges offer.

For example, find out if lower and upper-division courses are:

- Lecture and small lab format.
- Socratic method
- Learn-by-doing format
- Cooperative programs
- Independent capstone programs

Understanding how courses are offered will help clarify what makes each school unique, and which schools will support your learning style. Weighing the pros, cons, and trade-offs between large public universities, small liberal arts schools, polytechnic institutions, or art design schools is a natural part of determining the college that is best for you. You may see yourself at a particular type of college, and the thought of looking at large public universities or small private colleges may not be the direction you thought your college search would take. As you begin your college search, consider ways that you can expand your college experience and, at the same time, personalize it. One way to expand your college opportunities is to look for schools that are members of consortiums that allow for cross-enrollment between colleges.

If you want to take advantage of the depth, breadth, and resources in a larger research university, seek out schools that offer Honors Programs or have Learning-Living Communities.

Build a set of QUESTIONS to help you discover:

- How easy is it to cross-enroll with other local colleges or participate in shared programs? That may include understanding how much enrollment lead time, transportation needs, and other requirements.

- Are programs/courses offered only during the traditional school year i.e., fall, winter, and spring, or during summer as well?

- Are there additional costs, or is cross-enrollment already included in your tuition?

- Are Learning/Living communities specific to particular majors or interests? How long are you required to live in that community? Can you switch communities?

By being your own best college detective, it is possible to find the right mix of "big-small" - "small-big" educational environment for the college experience you want to have.

By being your own best college detective, it is possible to find the right mix of "big-small" - "small-big" educational environment for your college experience.

"likely"..."best fit"...or..."reach"
assess where schools fit for you.

I f you attend high school in California, applying to a UC seems like a natural step when putting together your college list. The UCs are public and have manageable tuition costs relative to many other schools. They offer a breadth of courses and activities, all within a short car, train, or plane ride home. While location, size of school, and depth of programs are qualities and priorities that can "jump-start" building your college list, determining if a school is in the "likely," "best fit," or "reach"[12] category is key to achieving a balanced college list. Building a balanced college list helps create a successful pathway to college and avoids schools that are dead ends. A balanced list also can aid in managing your application workload. While many public universities have higher acceptance rates, factoring in intended majors or academic areas (e.g., Computer Science) can make a huge difference in assessing if a school is "likely," "best fit," or "reach." For instance, if you are looking at other big public schools on the West Coast, the University of Washington, the University of Oregon, and Oregon State are excellent options with honors colleges, robust academic offerings, and a collegiate vibe. But suppose you're interested in, for example, Computer Science or STEM. In that case, while the University of Washington has exceptional Computer Science and STEM programs, its popularity in these areas equates to low out-of-state acceptance rates[13], so while some schools may be a "best fit" or "likely" in some majors, they can become a "reach" or "hail mary" based on major or if you're applying from out of state.

Numerous resources are available to help you determine where the UCs, or any other school, fit as you balance your college list, including College Data, Naviance, SCOIR, and each college's website. Each website offers a range of information, but looking at application requirements and admission stats will help you assess where you fit for admissions and provide a reliable comparison between you, and all admitted students. The other tool you will want to utilize, specifically for UC applicants, is the UC eligibility index[14] to determine whether you are UC eligible in

---

12 Grove, Allan. "Reach School in College Admissions." ThoughtCo., 2019
13 "Freshmen by the numbers | Office of Admissions." Office of Admissions
14 "Admissions index instructions." UC Admissions

the state-wide or local context.[15] With many UCs receiving over 100,000 applications each application cycle, even with the latest shifts to admit more in-state CA residents, there is no indication that the demand to attend[16]whether from California students, students outside of the state, or international students, will be diminishing anytime soon.

The article "Hey UC grads: Could you get into your alma mater to-day?"[17] underscores how the UCs have emerged as formidable, highly selective universities and can no longer be considered "likely" schools. While the UC system is comprised of nine large public schools that offer both undergraduate and graduate programs (UCSF offers graduate and professional studies), like all universities, they have capacity limitations.[18] As a result, when determining whether to include them on a college list, the best approach is to think of them individually and assess if they meet your criteria for college. Too often, the question "What does it take to get in?" comes up when starting the college search. Flipping that question to "Which schools will support what I want for my college experience?" will lead to a more successful college search and application process.

What can you do to build a balanced list? First, expand your view of the colleges to explore. Think broadly and beyond the familiar names while focusing on your key priorities for your college experience. Those might be driven by wanting any of several factors, including public vs. private university, specific location, curriculum, study abroad programs, internships, honors program, quality of recreational facilities for when you're not in class,

Taking advantage of college search tools like the CollegeData app, whether touring colleges in-person or virtually, can help you learn more about each college, the size of the school, what majors they offer, graduation rate, demographics, and requirements for applicants to assess fit for you.

15 "Local guarantee (ELC) | UC Admissions." UC Admissions
16 Watanabe, Teresa. "UC record college admission applications show wide diversity." Los Angeles Times, 29 January 2021
17 "Hey, UC grads: Could you get into your alma mater today?" KPCC, 23 March 2018
18 Freedberg, Louis. "California's public universities struggle with rising college eligibility." EdSource, 17 August 2017

cost to attend, athletics, or any other criteria specific to you. Start with ensuring that a school has what you want for your college experience.

Next, factor in whether an academic area or major that interests you is "impacted" or "capped" and will be a more competitive program for admission purposes. The CSUs are excellent public universities to explore, especially if you want to stay in California. Paying attention to which campuses, like Cal Poly San Luis Obispo, are heavily impacted[19] is important and may shift schools like Cal Poly into the category of "reach" schools similar to the UCs. Once you have those key components nailed down, you can look at acceptance rates to ensure that you have a mix of schools that admit a large portion of applicants rather than only highly selective/rejective schools with low admit rates. How do you do that? If you're looking for a Polytechnic school in CA, take the time to visit other Polytechnic schools, like the newest CSU Polytechnic – Humboldt, or look for schools with multiple majors that are in your areas of interest. Take a step to the right or left of what you were thinking about studying. Do you want to develop software or maintain IT systems? Are you interested in Environmental Science and research, or do you want to work on Environmental Policy? If you're interested in Business with a big B, are you also interested in Economics or Organizational Psychology and how companies work?

If you are working on building your list and cost affordability is essential, look for states that participate in an interstate reciprocal tuition program; for example, California and West Coast schools are part of the Western Interstate Commission for Education (WICHE) that have established cost-saving partnerships via WUE[20] which offer comparable tuition rates among colleges in their member states or may provide merit scholarships to bring the cost to attend closer to your home state tuition. In addition, you want to verify which schools are active, as some majors or schools may not participate.

Finally, ensure that you review a school's mission and what it is looking for in its applicants. High school graduation requirements may differ widely from the academic or additional requirements that each college/ university values and those requirements are not uniform among all universities and colleges. While you may not be able to determine

---

19 "Impaction." Cal Poly
20 "Welcome to Your WUE Savings Finder." WICHE

whether a school is, for example, looking for a saxophone player or to fill a specific major, learning what each school values will help you determine how you match up as you build your list of schools. Knowing how schools fit your interests, whether you are looking to stay in California, want a large public university, or are focused on college affordability, should be part of your process to achieve a balanced college list.

college.u
SOPHOMORE CHECKLIST

2. Get Involved. Join New Activities or Clubs

1. Build Interest, Rigor, and Balance into Your Class Schedule

3. Start Something New Based on Your Interests- Project, Club, Internship, or WHAT?

4.Do Things That Make You Happy

5. Plan for Summer

7. Make a Test Plan

6. Engage in Your Community

8. Get Good at Something You Love

9. Sign up for a PSAT or PreACT

10. Start to Build Your College Timeline

www.collegeu.solutions

"There are only two days in the year that
nothing can be done. One is called yesterday and
the other is called tomorrow,
so today is the right day to love, believe,
do and mostly live."

~ Dalai Lama

three

EXPANDING YOUR INTERESTS

investing in you

While getting sucked into the latest news on testing or admission rates is easy, investing in "you" remains the core tenet when applying to college. You are the one true thing that drives your college journey, and you are comprised of your likes and dislikes, the things that you are drawn to, the classes that you find fascinating, and the way you organize the hours in the day to do what's most important to you. So, when you ask yourself, "What should I be doing now to get into college?" the first step is to reframe that question and instead ask, "What interests me?", "How can I pursue those interests?" and "When and how can I do that?" Move away from checking boxes. Move away from doing what everyone else is doing. Yes, it may be better to partner up with a friend or group of friends if you're trying to start something new, help your community, or do a trail cleanup, but the common thread should be doing something that interests you. Of course, moving towards doing what is most important to you takes time and thought to enable you to seek ways and places to accomplish and achieve your ambitions. There is no set timeline on when to begin and how long it will take, so if you think you need to wait for your junior year of high school to start a passion project, that's not the case. Start when you're ready. Meaningful elements of investing in you require you to take the initiative, lead the charge, and map out your path. Start with a budding interest that can be nurtured into a project that is an investment in you. The possibilities are limitless, and you can turn your ideas into reality. While you may find a portal to your interests through high school clubs like Key Club, Student Government, or a buffet of organizations, look beyond the usual. Start with what excites you. That can range from looking back at an early fascination like digging up roly-polies in your backyard, playing a musical instrument, knowing the stats for your favorite sports teams, or taking care of a younger sibling. Take stock of what holds your attention. Have you spent the last 14 months deep in Minecraft, reorganizing your room, working out, or baking? Examine and break down why those activities held your attention. Did they allow you to form connections, collaborate, express your ingenuity, or see tangible or immediate results? Analyze the common themes that reflect your interests and their origins to help you think about how to develop them. Some of the most intriguing activities begin with a seed carried for years waiting to be planted so that it can grow into something formative.

"Do not follow where the path may lead. Go instead where there is no path and leave a trail." - Ralph Waldo Emerson

Do you have an idea waiting to be nudged into something meaningful to you, like the student who loved baking and started a cooking show or the soon-to-be journalist who created a news blog and pivoted it into a club at their high school? Or are you interested in a large-scale environmental project like the student that helped a community stop burning garbage by creating a communal compost system to reduce toxic emissions? Or do you need to find a quiet place to sit and read?

Using summer as your test kitchen can be the perfect way to explore, expand, and invest in yourself, develop your interests, and cook up a plan that is authentic to you. The possible ways to put your ideas into action range from taking a course to build your knowledge and academic foundation, initiating a project that connects with your community, or engaging in a self-study endeavor that may include introspection.

Stepping out of your comfort zone, sitting down to brainstorm the pos-sibilities, and charting out a plan may lead to finding new interests and developing skills for life, including:

- Communicating with multiple people and organizations

- Time management & prioritizing
- Leadership (which doesn't necessarily require a title)
- Collaboration & brainstorming
- Creativity
- Financial skills
- Organization & management
- Technology skills

Discovering precisely what you like may require time, guidance, and encouragement to jump into new experiences or challenges. Pursuing interests in a more focused way and giving yourself time to grow and see the world beyond your doorstep all require reflection to understand what you're experiencing. Investing in yourself throughout your college journey will help you take ownership of your choices, whether in the classes you take, activities you are drawn to, or ways you engage and learn about your community. This mindset will not only help you determine your path forward but also help you embrace your goals. The more you invest in yourself, the clearer your path will be.

....

community service: engaging in what matters to you

April is National Volunteer Month, but no rule says students need to wait until April to volunteer or start looking for projects they want to engage in. A month dedicated to supporting organizations tackling poverty, health, or environmental issues creates awareness about what nonprofits and NGOs do and can help students expand their world. Participating in programs that are a step out into a broader community allows students to help others and their communities and provides an opportunity [1] to examine their values surrounding empathy, altruism,

1   Kristof, Nicholas. "Opinion | The Four Secrets of Success." The New York Times, 7 December 2019

resilience, and persistence. Students come to the world of community service with varying degrees of enthusiasm and awareness of societal inequality and community service impacts. With that in mind, exploring varying types of volunteer opportunities, whether in your neighborhood, another part of the country, or outside of the U.S., can be a significant first step to discovering the power to create change on a local or global level.

"Service is the rent we pay for the privilege of living on this earth."

- James Baldwin

I am often asked, "When and where should I do community service?" and "How many hours do I need to do?". When just beginning to think about community service, these are excellent questions to ask and essential when considering timing and programs that will support a positive and impactful experience. However, the waters on community service get muddied when the questions come up late in high school and are tied directly to viewing community service as a prerequisite box that needs to be checked to apply to college successfully. For colleges trying to assess a student's character, one clue in their college application is the level of the student's engagement beyond their academic obligations. Students often feel that the only way to express this engagement is through big endeavors, such as voluntourism trips.

Voluntourism combines travel abroad with volunteer work. Though it is a trend that has recently caught the public eye, engaging with this popular form of community service can be a complex and slippery slope[2]. While voluntourism can be mutually beneficial to both the volunteer and the people served, sometimes the focus ends up falling disproportionately on building a resume for the volunteer, resulting in faulty short-term projects rather than promoting the long-term well-being of the community. Not only does voluntourism sometimes take advantage of the community, but it can also take away from a student's opportunity to create a truly meaningful experience. Why halfheartedly participate in a project in Guatemala when you could have a transformative experience simply volunteering at your local library? With proper research, students

2 Freidus, Andrea. "The problem with volunteer tourism for NGOs is it doesn't do much good." Quartz, 2017

can assess the legitimacy, positive and potentially harmful impacts, and cost of participating in a particular program to determine if it will meet their needs and goals for service.

What is sometimes overlooked is how students can demonstrate and articulate their core values in ways that may not include voluntourism trips. While many students might grab onto the one-week trip or international beach clean-up, they should not assume those are the only ways to demonstrate who they are and what they value. Not all students have the time to build a long-term commitment to single or multiple organizations. A good starting place can be small-scale and even short-term. Dipping a toe in the vast ocean of volunteer opportunities creates a means for students to discover where their interests lie. Students whose curiosity

So how do students begin and decide what community service opportunity is right for them? How do parents support them? Here are ten questions to answer to help form the right plan:

1. Do you like hands-on experiences and seeing tangible and immediate results?

2. How much time are you able to spend outside of school?

3. Do you like to travel or prefer being close to home?

4. How do you spend school breaks and summers?

5. Do you have an interest or talent to share with others?

6. Is there an age requirement to volunteer?

7. Do I need to make a regular ongoing commitment, or is there a drop-in option?

8. Will I be working directly with people or working behind the scenes?

9. Does the program occur in the summer, the school year, or all year?

10. Do you have an interest already, like: climate, food disparity, education, health, or something else you want to be more involved in, or do you want to explore a variety of projects?

about volunteering is just budding can explore local opportunities, like volunteering at a community library,[3] food bank,[4] or environmental group.[5]

I often hear the question, "Don't I have to volunteer to get into college?". My response is that volunteering shouldn't just be about your college application; it's an opportunity to engage with and help your community. It is up to you to define who and where your community is- within a five-mile radius of your home, in your state, in your country, or on another continent- just as long as those community members want your assistance.

-Determining a genuine interest- whether in a hands-on project, supporting an existing nonprofit, or working in a specific area- will make the difference in creating a meaningful community service experience that goes way beyond checking a box.

....

you are more than a test score

To test or not to test? If you're entering the world of college admissions, trying to understand the world of testing, determining whether tests are required or not, and discerning which colleges require standardized tests, which will review an AP score if you submit, and which offer test-optional or test-blind pathways may all seem like new territory. The debate between higher education professionals about whether test scores predict college success and whether test scores should be used in the admissions process has been going on for quite some time. The players include college admissions teams, professors, college counselors, high school counselors, folks at Fair Test, and ACT and College Board testing companies. Part of the discussion is focused on the assumption that test scores provide unequivocal empirical evidence of a student's intellectual ability as a predictor of student success. New data, including a recent study, tells a different story. If you have the time, read books like Paul Tough's "The Years That Matter Most: How College Makes or

---

3   "Volunteer." Oakland Public Library
4   Food is a basic human right. Help us end hunger in the bay Area., 5 October 2022
5   Mission Blue: Home

Breaks Us"[6] or Nicholas Lemann's "The Big Test: The Secret History of Meritocracy."[7] You will find that many admission professionals agree that test scores are not the magic formula to predict an applicant's ability and the likelihood of college success.

Over the last few years, several schools like the University of Chicago, Pitzer, and Cal Tech have either gone test-optional or dropped subject test requirements. (Sidenote: subject tests are no longer offered by College Board, so this issue is basically moot). WPI and Northern Illinois University are test-blind and took an early bold step that partly acknowledges test scores are not entirely necessary as predictors of college success. What does this mean for students and families trying to interpret the news on testing? How can students apply this information when thinking about taking standardized tests? When reviewing applications to assess if a student is a good fit for their school, colleges look for many attributes and data points to determine fit. Each college weighs various attributes differently depending on its academic mission. As an example, Notre Dame puts a greater emphasis on Religious Affiliation/Commitment versus State Residency.

In contrast, the University of Texas, Austin, weighs State Residency more heavily and does not consider Religious Affiliation/Commitment, Level of Applicant's Interest, or Interviews as part of their review process. Yes, strong scores are good, and yes, having the most robust score possible may get your foot in the door at Ivy League and similar schools. Still, it is just one piece of the puzzle rather than necessarily a piece that will significantly shift the overall review of an application.

Significantly, the primary data points that matter are GPA and rigor in coursework, not test scores. Test scores may underscore or mirror a student's mastery of their high school classes and serve as an exclamation point to their academic abilities. But GPA and test scores don't always align and often tell a story that requires a closer look at an applicant, including where the applicant attended high school, what curriculum the applicant studied, what the applicant did outside of school, and what the applicant values. This is when a holistic review of a student's application

---

6   Tough, Paul. The Years that Matter Most: How College Makes Or Breaks Us. Houghton Mifflin Harcourt, 2019
7   Lemann, Nicholas. The Big Test: The Secret History of the American Meritocracy. Farrar, Straus and Giroux, 2000

becomes essential. Many colleges utilize a holistic approach in their admissions review, and some colleges are now identifying attributes like character and community engagement as more important than test scores. The critical thing for students to remember is that standardized test scores are one data point in a college application, and Admission teams recognize this. Nonetheless, some more prominent public universities with large applicant pools still rely heavily on GPA and test scores. The primary data point still given the most weight to predict student college success remains GPA.

If you're a junior, you most likely have a testing plan in place or are working on developing one, including identifying which test to take, the best timing to take tests, and possibly exploring test-optional routes. If you are an underclassman, you may be starting to think about standardized tests and where they fit in your college timeline. While many schools continue to move toward test-optional options, determining if that option applies to you requires understanding several specific factors, including your strengths and abilities and the colleges you are considering.

One of the important stories that shifted the direction of testing require-ments was the UC Academic Senate Special Task Force review and the UCs' response, leading the UCs and CSUs to adopt a test-blind policy. Even with this significant change, school requirements are not uniform and may adjust after each admission cycle, as is the case with MIT now requiring test scores. Assessing if taking a test is moot is difficult to gauge for a student early in their college journey. The best plan is to pay attention and stay the course. Most high school students can still expect that developing a test plan specific to them will be the best route to keep options open and help avoid last-minute scrambling and missed dead-lines. As the admissions process evolves and the weight of standardized tests shifts, maintaining flexibility and keeping your eyes on the road ahead will ensure that you have the most robust application that reflects the multiple facets of who you are. You are more than a test score when applying to college.

....

ACT vs. SAT? accommodations?

The Varsity Blues Scandal[8] revealed that requests for accommodations could be manipulated to give an unfair advantage to students who don't need accommodations. For students with true testing issues requiring accommodations, navigating how to secure accommodations can be critical and time-sensitive. Determining if you qualify for accommodations includes understanding what factors are considered, what documentation is needed, and how long the process will take to receive accommodation approval. For students that do not qualify for accommodations but still find standardized tests do not reflect their abilities or college readiness, building in test-optional schools is a pathway that should not be overlooked. The big takeaway: start early, make a plan, and get your documentation ducks in a row.

RESOURCES, ARTICLES AND VIDEOS

- "Accommodations Requests: SAT vs. ACT,"[1] Matt Steiner, M.A.

- Affluence and Accommodations: Wealthier Students are Securing More School-based Accommodations for Disabilities,[2] Dr. Jed Applerouth, Ph.D.

- Standardized Testing and Students with Disabilities,[3] FairTest

- ACT Announces Section Retesting, Superscore Reporting, and Online Testing, Compass Prep[4]

1 Steiner, Matty. "Accommodations Requests: SAT vs. ACT." Compass Education Group, July 1, 2022

2 Applerouth PhD, Jed. "Affluence and Accommodations: Wealthier Students are Securing More School-based Accommodations for Disabilities." August 13, 2019. Applerouth,

3 "Standardized Testing and Students with Disabilities." Fairtest, 2017. Fairtest

4 Sawyer, Art. "ACT Announces Section Retesting, Superscore Reporting, and Online Testing." 2019. Compass Education Group,

8 Korn, Melissa, and Jennifer Levitz. Unacceptable: Privilege, Deceit & the Making of the College Admissions Scandal. Penguin Publishing Group, 2020

tracing your digital footsteps

Have you opened your inbox recently to discover a slew of emails from colleges? Thinking about your digital footprints, social media, and how they connect to your college search and admissions process is another piece of the college application puzzle. Are colleges tracking you? In a world of interconnection, living in the open, and sharing aspects of our personal lives, may require guidelines, particularly for high school or college students asserting their place in the world. Simply stated, a digital life as an extension of your story requires intentional thought about what and why to share.

Creating social media accounts can provide an opportunity to share activities and projects and connect with others with similar interests. It also may be a chance to expand views and conversations. With online group and community activities that do not have the added visual cue of face-to-face interaction, knowing the rules or etiquette can make online connections meaningful and help avoid misconstrued or potentially inflammatory rhetoric. Extending your world and community can be a positive opportunity, but creating a false persona or inventing a personal brand is not the goal. Recognizing that your digital life is an extension of yourself and your character is only one aspect of the college application process. Recognizing that your digital life is an extension of yourself, and your character is only one aspect of the college application process. Not every student has an online presence, and in fact, it isn't a prerequisite to apply to college. Who you are is something college admissions teams want to know. And there are many avenues to conveying what makes you "you," so if you aren't interested or haven't created any social media accounts, staying off the grid is more than o.k. If you've signed up for a college newsletter, or summer program, or toured a college, you won't be too surprised if you get emails and letters from those schools. If you registered to take the SAT or ACT, you also might start receiving emails and correspondence from schools not on your radar. What you may not realize is what test companies do with your information.[9] Registering your email with SAT or ACT and not opting out of sharing your information cuts both ways. On the one hand, receiving information from a broad

9 Boeckenstedt, Jon. "College Board changing Student Search™: The thing we're all missing." Jon Boeckenstedt's Admissions Weblog, 4 April 2023

range of colleges can help expand a student's view of schools to consider when starting their college search. On the other hand, it also means students need to be savvy and recognize that just because they receive an email from "XYZ College" doesn't guarantee they will be accepted.

So what are some parameters for your online life beyond the golden rule of "don't post or share something you would not want your Grandmother to see"?

- Are family and friends part of your digital footprint because they post and share information about you? And, if so, does it align with how you see yourself and want others to see you?

- When does posting become oversharing?

- Consider what types of conversation broaden discussions and when something should be shared privately.

- Consider using the 10-10-10 rule and how you might feel about a post.

- You may think you have a private account, but having followers with a public account may provide a backdoor for others to see your social media accounts.

While many colleges do not have the time or resources to review every applicant's social media accounts, many schools do, and that number is ticking up. Suppose something questionable is inconsistent with the character of what a student has asserted themselves to be. In that case, a college may rescind their offer or move an application into the "deny" pile. Conversely, you may have a project of particular interest that lives on the internet that you want to showcase.

Connection to the world, building community, and sharing opinions online can be an opportunity for positive impact in a light-hearted or purposeful way. While smartphone posts and tweets are often created in the palm of your hand or on a laptop screen, they still are part of a two-way communication process. While there may not be a group of people peering through your phone or laptop camera at any given moment, you can be sure anything you post will be seen and become part of your digital footprints. So, what else do you need to know as you enter the world of social media?

Luckily there is no shortage of advice for high school and college students, and the articles below provide more guidance for what you need to know.

- Colleges Mine Data on Their Applicants[10]
- 8 Ways to Better Navigate the Internet in 2020[11]

....

10 Belkin, Douglas. "Colleges Mine Data on Their Applicants." Wall Street Journal, 2019,
11 Herrera, Tim. "8 Ways to Better Navigate the Internet in 2020." The New York Times, 26 December 2019

college.u
JUNIOR CHECKLIST

2. College Visits & College Fairs

1. Self-Assessments

3. Start Exploring Educational Priorities

4. Identify SAT/ACT Timing & Prep

5. Research/ Building College List

7. Resume & Track Activities

6. Demonstrated Interest

8. Finish Taking Standardized Tests

9. Secure Recommendation Letters

10. Start Personal Essay Draft

www.collegeu.solutions (C)(TM)

"And now let us welcome a new year

full of things that never were."

-Rainer Marie Rilke

four

your essays. your voice. your words.

Your authentic voice is the key to unlocking a successful essay. You've probably heard that a few hundred times, but what does that really mean? Don't write from 30,000 feet above ground hiding behind clichés and well-worn phrases. Make your essay personal so that no one else could have written it. Write about what is core to you. Be specific, be pithy, be inventive. Beware of the semi-colon unless you have a black belt in grammar. Embrace time as a trusted friend and make sure you have built in plenty of hours to ponder, cogitate, draft and re-draft. Read your essay aloud. Does it sound like you or what you think someone wants to hear? Admissions committees want to hear your voice, idiosyncrasies, tone, rhythm, and take on the world. Take this opportunity to speak loudly and directly. The best first step sometimes is to start writing and find out what you have to say.

Looking for inspiration? Richard Hugo's book "The Triggering Town: Essays and Lectures on Poetry and Writing."[1] offers tips that hold weight for tackling not just poetry but good writing, which is where the college essay needs to live.

....

1   Hugo, Richard. The Triggering Town: Lectures And Essays On Poetry And Writing. WW Norton, 2010

- "Tell Colleges You Love Them,"[1] Willard Dix, Forbes

- "My Very Unofficial Tips on Writing Your College Essay,"[2] Dan Milaschewski, Harvard

- "Hearing the Voice of a 51-Year-Old Man in the Essay of a 17-Year-Old Girl,"[3] Rachel Toor, New York Times

- "6 Things You Should Never Do As the Parent of a College Applicant,"[4] Ann Brenoff

---

1 Dix, Willard. "Tell Colleges You Love Them." Forbes, 2017

2 Milaschewski, Dan. "My Very Unofficial Tips on Writing Your College Essay,." Harvard College Blog, 2016

3 Toor, Rachel. "Hearing the Voice of a 51-Year-Old Man in the Essay of a 17-Year-Old Girl." The New York Times Web Archive, 19 October 2010

4 Brenoff, Ann. "6 Things You Should Never Do As the Parent of a College Applicant." Huffpost, 2015

Unicorn or Troll

Too often, students and families think of the college essay as the elusive unicorn that, if slayed, will magically get a student into college. Rather the truth of writing college essays is that you, the student, are the unicorn, and your essay is the map that connects the dots for your reader to find you in the forest of other college applicants. What also has become muddied for students and families is the presumption that there is a need for a certain kind of story or specific experiences that will provide subject matter for college essays. When, in fact, embracing a Nora Ephron mantra, "everything is copy," coupled with reflection, time, and a few essay exercises, a student's stories will surface in a way that connects their dots genuinely and honestly in their voice. Knowing this early on before beginning the application and essay phase is vital so as students explore or deepen their interests, their essays are specific to who they are rather than fabricated, ghost-written or computer generated. Reading some of the recent AI-generated essays as writers, journalists, and students are curious about how AI can be employed as a tool, and reading a number of those AI-generated essays has put a finer point on what is generic and impersonal. While serviceable, the loss of a student's voice, their idiosyncratic eccentricities, the temptation and use of AI for essays seem like a troll sucking out the very essence of what makes them a unicorn.

Thinking about your essays and stories and which ones are the most compelling often leads to the question, "should I be doing something to strengthen my application to college, so I have something to write about?" While this is a reasonable question, it is not necessarily the best question. Your story will be the platform for connecting the dots of what's important to you, what you value, and how you spend your time. Deepening or expanding an interest because you can't help yourself, having a natural curiosity driving or fuels you should be the impetus. Yes, you may have more experiences to draw from, but fabricating an activity to have a story should not be the motivation. Every few years, activities that once were unique or one-offs turn into a trending wave, whether it's a summer internship, starting a company, or camp, etc. These can be awesome projects if they are entirely student-driven, from IG accounts to stapled flyers in a neighborhood and originate in a student's deep interest. As content for college essays or applications, they are not necessarily needed and can come off flat or one of the same kind of essay. Writing college essays is not the tail that wags the dog. The best stories and activities are the ones that start with a student's fascination, and often, those have been building over time. While taking a seed of early interest and growing and nurturing it into something more meaningful through extracurricular or summer activities is valuable and should not be diminished, checking where the motivation comes from will help stay true to what makes a student a true unicorn and not a troll.

landing your college essays

One way to think about college essays is that they are interviews on paper. Now imagine sitting down to meet your potential employer for the first time. You might have prepared for your interview by learning about the company and what skills the job entails so you can talk about your skills, like the ability to adapt and learn quickly. You probably will want to convey your excitement for the opportunity to grow with their company. You might even have a list of questions that show you know their business niche, products, and how they work with clients.

You want to use this same approach when writing college essays and demonstrate through your writing:

- Your specific strengths and abilities.
- Demonstrate a positive and can-do attitude. It sounds a little old-school but showing that you have initiative and follow-through are qualities that can lead to success and what employers value.
- Excellent communication skills.

Communicating is integral to any interview and even more critical to writing a college essay. A succinct and reflective essay will address the question ("prompt") being asked and demonstrate your ability to understand and read between the lines. While many college essay prompts seem open-ended, the questions are, in fact, seeking specific information of interest to the interviewer/college. It is your job to figure out what that is.

Writing clear and concise essays and answering the essay prompt is akin to sitting across a desk from the person who may be determining your future path. You want to convey why you are the best candidate, how your academic and extracurricular choices have been intentional, and how they will be an asset to the college you are applying to. Focusing on what you have done and how that will translate to the future, even when applied to a different activity, field, or major, is part of sharing what makes you unique and essential in writing college essays.

Just as you will highlight your strengths and skills in an interview, you probably want to avoid areas that might put doubt in your potential employer's mind. You might not start an interview by saying you need time off or write in your essay about 1) wanting to take a Gap year, 2) expressing uncertainty about attending college in general, or 3) mentioning other colleges you are interested in. While these may be things you are thinking about, put them in your thought bubble, and keep your focus on the task at hand, conveying your interest or commitment as an intentional applicant. If the job has specific requirements, would you begin by sharing an issue that may impact your ability to do the job? In this same way, writing about an issue that is potentially a red-flag topic may be more about providing context for personal success and steps to overcoming a challenge than solely about the challenge.

"You don't start out writing good stuff. You start out writing crap and thinking it's good stuff, and then gradually, you get better at it. That's why I say one of the most valuable traits is persistence."
-Octavia E. Butler

The strength and perseverance to overcome a health or life challenge is extraordinary and should not be dismissed; one question to consider is where that story fits best when applying to college. If attending school or participating in extracurricular activities were impacted or limited, you should include details to give context in the Additional Information section, a supplemental essay, or for this year in the COVID supplemental essay.

Writing about overcoming difficult life and health challenges in your college essay requires answering questions that may be in the admissions rep's mind, like:

- How does this aspect of your life fit with all the other compelling pieces of who you are?

- What were the steps you took or implemented to be successful?

- Did this impact your ability to attend a school or your grades, and if so, how did you address this?

- How did this challenge shape who you are today?

The college essay helps colleges know your individual characteristics and life circumstances. Finding the best place to highlight your unique qualities should be intentional and just as important as choosing your Personal Statement topic or story. Highlighting your strengths, framing them, and giving them the weight they deserve is not limited to your Personal Statement. Taking advantage of all the essay opportunities involves work and more writing, but it is an investment in revealing all aspects of your character and what you value. There is no way to predict 100% of the outcome during the admissions process or applying for a job. Writing essays that translate what defines you so your reader hears your voice, understands your ideas and intentions clearly, and sees that you are ready to attend college are things you can control in your college journey.

....

the key piece in the application puzzle

There are many pieces to the college application puzzle – not quite 1000, but enough pieces are required to provide a college admissions team a picture of who you are, share what you value, and the direction you are headed. Approaching the application season might seem impossible to make sense of how all the pieces will fit, but one piece of the puzzle that may have even greater importance is the opportunity to tell your story.

With the "flattening of grades" when some high schools moved to pass/ fail models or disruption in activities, you want an opportunity to share your progress, nimbleness, and triumphs. There is a place for this in your applications, and colleges provide additional opportunities for you to write about what you have achieved and experienced. An upward trend (or hiccup) in grades and success in the classroom is important to convey but does not need to be the overarching theme of essays. You are multi-dimensional, and painting a clear and multi-colored image for your reader will be more compelling and keep them engaged. Yes, providing academic details to give a broader context of academics is essential, but just as school is not your only interest, the essay should not be one-dimensional.

At the very heart of any college essay is -- well, the heart of you. This does not mean the essay should aim to be a "sob story," as one of my students called it a few years back. What it does mean is that you need to write about things that are so central to what defines you, using your words, syntax, and sentence rhythms that, when read, it is as if you are sitting across the room telling it to your reader.

Some of the most successful stories often start with something small and seemingly impersonal. The trick can be in the telling. Sometimes a story weaves lessons learned, aspirations, or observations that emphasize the depth of character that might not easily be seen in your daily life and other parts of your application. Some students can access a well of robust language, while others will rely on words that are spare and clear. Stitching together an essay that shouts or sings quietly, a statement of "I am here" is part of the work that makes the essay and application process transformative.

It will be tempting to write about what it was like to be a high school student, student-athlete, life-changing volunteer trip, or being sidelined during Covid. Before committing to any essay, remember that the world of rising seniors experience many of the same things. While it is true that each student's story will be unique, taking the time to ask if this is truly the most unique experience of your life can guide you to the core of who you are – and that is whom admission readers want to meet in your essay. It will be tempting for parents or family members to want to help, but this is the time for everyone to sit on their hands. Let the brainstorming and writing process take over. Writing essays can take weeks and sometimes months to form into a draft that will find its final form. Telling your story built on details and heart and revealing your character and aspirations will bring all the pieces together and put who you are at the center of what's most

....

revising in batches

I recently spent a weekend making batches of doughnuts. You may wonder why. I became fascinated with creating the right mix of flour, leavening, eggs, baking powder, or yeast with a delicious dusting of cinnamon and sugar.

Making batches of doughnuts reminded me of writing and revising college essays. You are probably thinking: of course, she would say that. What I found fascinating in my grand experiment that took over the entire kitchen multiple times was that I discovered how I really wanted my doughnuts to taste with each new variation on a recipe. There was, of course, the easy batch for beginners, with no rolling or rising involved. Truthfully, they were baked, not fried, so there was no drama. However, while my household and I gobbled them up and loved the cake-like texture and hints of nutmeg, we all missed the slightly golden crunch that comes from biting into a deep-fried doughnut[2]. This led me to my next revision of creating a homemade doughnut. In my initial batch, I opted for buttermilk and eggs. I like the richness that buttermilk adds to the dough and texture, so I knew I wanted to stick with that as a moistening component, but it was time to advance the cooking process and dive into the oil. Frying can be tricky. The right temperature, time in the oil, and paying close attention are key, as taking your eyes away for even a moment can morph a caramel-colored doughnut into a blackened blob.

It's no different when writing and revising essays. There are often places where you can switch out or add a word to clarify what you mean, and sometimes adding an entirely new idea can help move your essay to a place that expands what you want to say. As a developing writer or baker, giving yourself time to experiment is often the magic ingredient needed to land on the precise mix of words that makes your reader hungry to read your essay down to the last delicious bite.

For batch three, it was time to try a yeast concoction. The smell of yeasted dough rising is exquisite, and the trick of not sabotaging the rise is in the kneading, whether the recipe demands kneading, rolling, or none. Overworking the dough, like too much help when making final revisions, runs the risk of killing off all your hard work. Too much outside, albeit well-intended, advice can shift your best writing into something other than writing that reflects your ideas or how you would tell your story. It may look beautiful, but the heart of what you want to say may collapse under the weight of an outside expectation.

In arriving to reach my baking project goal of mastering homemade doughnuts, I realized that tackling multiple batches[3] was just the beginning. With each revised recipe, I would become more familiar with the chemistry between eggs, buttermilk, and baking powder, and thankful when the yeast began to grow.

---

2   Bittman, Mark. "Doughnuts Recipe - NYT Cooking." NYT Cooking,
3   "Doughnut Recipes & Menu Ideas | Bon Appétit." Bon Appetit

Writing college essays is also learning how to grow your ideas into something meaningful and thoughtful. The more you write, the more familiar you will be with how to say what you're thinking, which words sound like you, and how to order your ideas to help your reader see your thinking and not be left in chaos. While having a set recipe or rules might be a starting place when baking or writing, you want to give yourself time to develop what will ultimately have your golden stamp of approval.

12 TIPS FOR WRITING COLLEGE ESSAYS

DO

- Like a fingerprint, sharing a story from your distinct viewpoint in a way no one else could ever write will leave your imprint and define your essay as yours. You are a one-of-a-kind original. Take the time to brainstorm topics and ideas you want to share to help the admissions committee see you.

- Write in your 17-year-old voice. While humor can be entertaining, sarcasm and slang do not always translate. Including words and phrases you use daily and how you speak will make your essays sound like you.

- Remember who your audience is. Think of your essay as a way to invite them into your world. Admissions representatives are well-read essay readers with limited time. They've read 1000s of essays, so avoid cliches and overused metaphors. Do the originality check. If the story you are thinking about writing: a) reminds you of something you have read, b) you heard that a senior two years ago wrote about that topic, or c) falls into the 'how you were changed by volunteering on a service trip' category, think twice about writing what may be a well-worn story.

- Be specific. Include details. Make your story tactile (think five senses). Draw your admissions reader into your world. Writing big ideas can work if you ground them in concrete examples.

- Be confident. You can write your essay. Think of your essay as an interview on paper. What do you want schools to know about you? Tell the admissions representatives your story.

- If you need support, find someone you trust with expertise in college essays and who has the time to help- - that could be a high school college counselor, a writing workshop professional, an online essay expert, or an essay coach. Determine if you need one or multiple reviews to ensure you have the support you need and are not left out in the cold during application season.

- When finalizing your essays, read them out loud, and check for spelling, grammar, and details. Have someone put a second set of eyes on your essays for spelling, grammar, and sentence flow before submitting them. Spell-check does not catch everything. Typically, most seniors find someone other than their parents to do a final read.

DON'T

- If you write about a challenge, make sure to shift the focus onto steps you took to overcome or address the problem. An essay about a challenge is a moment to show your resilience, grit, and character.

- Avoid typical tropes: the final seconds in the championship game, writing about a family member (admissions representatives want to know who you are, not Auntie Jo), or even what you learned from Harry Potter. While Harry Potter books are the cherished book series for an entire generation, tread carefully when choosing how to write about your connection to them, whether that be what you learned about raising dragons from Hagrid or the bias Hermione experienced as a Muggle and how it relates to your life. Writing and defining your perspective in a meaningful and unique way is part of the challenge and will ultimately distinguish you from the crowd.

- Strong verbs, interesting nouns, a smattering of adjectives, and correct punctuation can create momentum and rhythm in a story. What usually falls flat is indulging in the temptation of the thesaurus. If you don't use a word in daily conversation, college essays are not the time to insert a $10 word. The caveat--if you do have a robust vocabulary, corral your desire to build a cornucopia of over-written sentences, and be sure to include space, pauses, and punctuation that lets your reader soak in the complexity of your essay and who you are.

- It will be tempting to have your family brainstorm or edit. You live with them. They have known you your entire life. They may remember a particular story that they feel defines you. There are ways parents and family members can support you, but ultimately you should decide what story to tell. This is your essay to write and your time to shine. Admissions representatives want to hear your authentic voice, not a fabricated or branded version of yourself - and after years of reading essays, they can tell the difference.

- While your early-on focus should be on developing your essay, spelling, and punctuation, any off-color words can undercut your writing and what you're trying to say. Finally, remember to proof, proof, proof.

too many cooks
in the college essay kitchen

Application season can be a touchy time as nerves rattle and worry percolates with impending deadlines. This is true not just for students but also for parents who are moving away from their role of manager to consultant. It wouldn't be a college essay season without the question of "How many cooks need to be in the kitchen?" When tackling the Personal Statement and Supplemental essays, a student's ultimate goal is to write their own essays about things that matter to them, told in their voice. Yet, students may flounder at the start, unfamiliar with the narrative form of the personal essay, and may need guidance on writing in a way that may feel more exposed than usual. Helping students balance highlighting what is core to them and specifically about them while not sounding boastful requires time and a seasoned guide. While some students may have access to an essay workshop, "how-to" books, English class, or essay coach, others may drift as they wrestle with where to begin and what to share. That uncertainty is okay - initially. Grappling with what to write about and how to write college essays is as central as the completed essays and, in some ways, more critical.

Patience, pondering, and tenacity are skills needed to write college essays; embracing these skills will empower students. While there may be an inclination for both students and parents to want to collaborate, Adrienne Wichard-Edds' article, "Experts offer four reasons why kids need to own their college essays — and one-way parents can help,"[4] underscores that the place to come together is around trust; students need to trust their instincts when writing and parents need to trust that their kids are more than capable of writing their own essays.

> "Writing is really a way of thinking — not just feeling but thinking about things that are disparate, unresolved, mysterious, problematic or just sweet."
> -Toni Morrison-

Even the most exquisite writers have a second set of eyes, a trusted mentor, or an editor reviewing their work before pronouncing it finished. High

---

4 Wichard-Edds, Adrienne. "Experts offer four reasons why kids need to own their own essays-and one-way parents can help." Washington Post, 13 October 2020

school seniors writing college essays should be no different, and a "light touch" from a trusted guide can make the difference between a well-written essay and a missed opportunity. Supporting students during the essay phase of the application process can take many forms, from creating a low-stress atmosphere to helping seniors pivot away from difficult conversations about college. While students do the heavy lifting when applying to college, family support can lighten the load and is a time for parents to break out of the comfort food and create levity balanced with calm.

Here are seven tips to consider while waiting for college essays to be fully baked.

TIP ONE: "We"[1] are not going to college, and "we" will not be writing papers in college. A student's ability to write essays may be one of many litmus tests for college readiness or possibly college fit for a student.

TIP TWO: "Too many cooks in the kitchen" often leave a student confused and caught in the middle of whose advice to take.

TIP THREE: Writing college essays is a moment where support is about empowering students to know and trust their instincts and their voice. Remember, a senior has 17 or 18 years of life experience to draw from, not 30. Sharing their insights from their perspective is essential and provides clues to understanding what they want to write about, what they know, and what they value.

TIP FOUR: Unsolicited help, the heavy use of a red pen, and suggestions on what to include from outside editors can often leave an essay over-seasoned, burnt, and inedible.

TIP FIVE: While the possibility of a college outright rejecting essays based on the DDI rule (Daddy Did It)[2] may be an urban myth, this is not the time to be a test case. Be aware that in recent years,[3] colleges have moved to use technology similar to "turn-it-in.com"[4] to sort out plagiarized writing.

1 Barnard, Brennan. "The Royal "We" in College Admission." 2018. Forbes
2 Schworm, Peter. "College applications can be too good - The Boston Globe." Boston.com, 12 February 2008
3 Zeveloff, Julie. "APPLICANTS BEWARE: Colleges Are Now Running Your Admissions Essays Through Plagiarism Software." 2012. Insider
4 Gordon, Larry. "When college applicants plagiarize, Turnitin can spot them." Los Angeles Times, 29 January 2012

TIP SIX: An essay's success can sometimes get muddled with the aspiration of applying to a highly selective school, which may require more complex writing and analytical thinking. If a student struggles to write a compelling essay or is missing the mark in their topic choice or tone, this is likely the time to pause and reflect on whether aspirations align with abilities. A ghost-written essay (which is at the very least unethical)[5] may foster the idea that essays and applications are all about "getting in," but the bigger question that needs to be answered is: if you can't write the essay, will you be able to write successfully in college.

TIP SEVEN: In a year when many colleges are test-optional, and the option to compare test scores to writing is limited, colleges still can compare high school courses taken to see if they align with the level of writing in submitted essays.

---

5 "Application affirmations." Common App

....

what colleges want to know about you

I know what you did… or at least that's what the UC said when they recently reminded counselors that they use plagiarism software. Of course, the idea that a student will plagiarize or have more than the usual help may seem foreign to you, but just a heads up, it's not only the UCs that care about who is actually writing the application essays. Aside from the obvious, colleges care for a variety of reasons. Many schools are being explicitly clear that the use of ChatGPT, Co-Pilot, Minerva, Photo Math to name a few are off limits.

The most important reason is that they want to hear a student's voice and, to the extent possible, get to know who a student is and what matters to them. Schools are not necessarily looking for pristine essays, and while there is a debate as to whether they can tell if an essay was written by a 45-year-old parent with 20+ years of writing experience, or plucked off the internet, why even risk it? Students often spend an exorbitant amount of time writing college essays because writing takes time, but keeping in mind that the essay is just one piece of the application can lower the pressure so that your words flow. Often the essay may not even be the most critical factor. Submitting the best piece of writing does take time, and not lowering standards as to how it's achieved is as important as the final product.

So what are some TIPS if you're writing college essays? ✓

- Avoid the humble brag, name-dropping, or repeating activities already listed in your essay or application.

- Lead by example when writing a leadership essay. Admission readers will see if you're Valedictorian, Captain, Manager, etc., but they might not know what responsibilities the role entailed or what skills you possess that contributed to the success of your school, team, and fellow workers. Focus on what you did, not the title.

- Develop your Demonstrated Intentionality, which means showing the college you know its mission and how it syncs up with your goals.

- Try to avoid repeating what has already been stated. Introduce something new. Building on an earlier idea in an essay can add depth and clarity.

- Write for your reader. Put yourself in their shoes. Imagine them sprawled on their couch, their favorite snack almost gone, it's nearly midnight, and they still have 30 more applications to read. What would you want to read?

- Choose your editor or final reviewer wisely. Pick someone who will let your voice shine through and provide feedback on areas that might need to be clarified or grammar that needs to be corrected so you can adjust and fully own your words.

Looking for more tips to help you through application season? Try these posts:

- The College Essay: Tips to Build the Best "Story of You" [1]
- Ugh, I Have to Write Another Essay?[2]
- Procrastination[3]
- Let's talk about interviews[4]
- Four Ways to Beat College Application Stress[5]

1 "The College Essay: Tips to Build the Best "Story of You." Ursinus College
2 "Ugh, I Have to Write Another Essay? – Colleges That Change Lives." Colleges That Change Lives
3 "Procrastination – The Writing Center • University of North Carolina at Chapel Hill." UNC Writing Center
4 Cao, Melissa. "Let's talk about interviews." MIT Admissions, 24 October 2022
5 "Four Ways to Beat College Application Stress - UIUC Admissions Blog." UIUC Admissions Blog, 11 October 2022

7 tips to break
the writer's block blues

The process of writing can sometimes seem mysterious, complex, and daunting. Just like training your body to run a race, writing essays takes time and practice (think drafting, editing, and polishing). It's easy to want to avoid the tired legs and sore muscles that come with pushing your body to start running or tackling a new distance, but the more you run (write), the stronger, more agile, and more successful you will become.

"Write what should not be forgotten." —Isabel Allende

Yes, writing may be hard, and working to be the kind of writer you want may take time and practice, but it is an attainable goal. The whole point is not to avoid writing or succumbing to the myth that you're not good at it or that it's too hard. It's all about building up your writing muscles and your ability to put your thoughts on the page.

- Journaling is a good way to build the habit of expressing yourself through writing without the pressure of creating polished work. Similar to starting to run or training for a race, finding your starting pace and not overloading yourself. Not much of a writer? Try journaling once a week for 15 minutes tops.

- Increase the days you write. Work up from one day to a few days to possibly every day. Set a schedule that works for you and commit to a particular time you want to write each day.

- Don't limit yourself in what you write about. Start with what interests you. It's true; we write best what we know. Create a set of pre-determined questions to answer each time you write, or write whatever comes to mind—venting into your notebook about the tough stuff counts. The key is getting pen to paper, fingers on the keyboard, and thumbs to the screen.

- What can you do if you get stuck? Copy. Do not steal or plagiarize, but find a piece of writing (the sports page, a grocery list, or even a recipe) and start copying it. Keep copying until you find your own more interesting words and thoughts. You'd be surprised how copying can quickly pivot a person into writing something more compelling.

- Read your writing out loud to yourself or a trusted soul. Try telling the rest of the story out loud. If you can, take notes or tell your story to someone else to capture your tone, intonation, and rhythm of your voice.

- Write a letter. Pick your audience-someone you like and will want to hear what you have to say.

- Don't edit as you go or worry about the minutiae (grammar, sentence flow, clarity) when you want to get your thoughts on the page. No one said the words must come together perfectly on the first try. Editing as you write will unnecessarily weigh you down and dishearten you. Can't think of the right word? Write down the closest thing and make a note so you can return to it later. Capturing one imperfectly articulated thought is worth much more than not writing anything—and you'll thank yourself later.

college.u
SENIOR CHECKLIST

1. Finalize College List

2. Calendar Application Deadlines

3. College Contacts, Attend Rep Visits

4. Personal Essay

5. Secure Recommendation Letters

6. Update Resume

7. Supplemental Essays

8. Submit Test Scores & FAFSA

9. Applications

10. Submit

www.collegeu.solutions

"Never be limited by other people's limited imaginations."

-Mae Jemison

five

demonstrated interest
- who cares?

College touring is another way to help determine which schools should end up on your college list and where you will ultimately go. College touring, while valuable, is not for everyone. If you want to visit only schools where you've been accepted, there are plenty of other ways to research upfront and demonstrate your interest in a particular school. Part of your research should include understanding if a school cares about Demonstrated Interest. The landscape is changing. Schools like Carnegie Mellon[1] no longer incorporate Demonstrated Interest when evaluating applicants. This shift reminds everyone that college visits are for prospective applicants to learn about what a college offers. Sign up for the official tour and information session. Build in the time to ask your tour guide or admissions representative questions that will help you assess if their school will support your aspirations. In addition to hosting information sessions for visiting prospective students, colleges often offer students an option to interview on campus or with Alumni. Finding out whether Interviews are a significant part of your applicant profile or purely informational will help you know whether you need to sign up in advance of your visit or schedule an interview in your hometown.

---

1 "Admission Consideration - Undergraduate Admission." Carnegie Mellon University

Regardless of when you tour, defining the nuances between curriculums, study abroad programs, housing, and other vital criteria important to you will support better decision-making for choosing schools, whether at the beginning or the end of your college search.

Not all liberal arts colleges, public universities, or highly selective schools have uniform institutional missions and campus environments. Walking on a college campus, meeting students, professors, and coaches, and taking an official tour will solidify the college search fact-finding and provide a sense of place and scale and the hands-on, realistic experience that most students need to determine their fit.

- In College Admissions, Is It Important To Show Your Love?[2]
- 'Demonstrated Interest' Is Really Time-Consuming [3]
- Colleges Mine Data on Their Applicants[4]

....

interview tips

Interviews can count. As much as the interview should be relaxed and friendly, keep in mind that Interviewers are gauging whether you will fit well into their college.

Alumni often do interviews, can be of different ages, and have other professions and varying backgrounds. Alums are typically unpaid and donate their time to meet with prospective students. Be respectful of their time.

Interviews primarily serve two purposes 1) to market their school and 2) to assess whether you would be a good fit for their school.

CONTACT- Typically, you will receive an email to set up a meeting time. Getting back to the Interviewer quickly will help demonstrate your interest in their school. If you are offered several time slots to meet and have a conflict, refrain from giving them all the details of your conflict,

---

2 Berler, Nina. "In College Admissions, Is It Important To Show Your Love?" 2019. Forbes

3 Reed, Matt. "Demonstrated Interest' Is Really Time-Consuming." Inside Higher Ed, 2018

4 Belkin, Douglas. "Colleges Mine Data on Their Applicants - WSJ." The Wall Street Journal, 26 January 2019

but rather explain that you have a prior commitment and ask if there is an alternate time to meet.

LOCATION- Interviews can occur on campus, at a local coffee shop, virtual, or someplace public vs. being invited into someone's home.

TIMING- Plan to arrive early. This will allow you to get a table or place to meet to provide a quiet setting. The Interviewer may offer to buy you a cup of coffee, etc. It is up to you to accept or decline, but remember you will be talking and want to avoid talking with your mouth full of food, spilling, etc. When the Interviewer arrives, stand if you are sitting, make eye contact, smile, and shake their hand firmly (no bone-breaking grips). Thank them for their time.

WHAT TO WEAR- Think of this as a job interview. You want to be yourself and let your Interviewer know you are serious about their school. Your clothes should be tidy, with no holes, rips, wrinkles and probably no tennis shoes. A coat and tie are optional, and a pressed shirt and slacks should be fine. Dress, skirt or slacks and shirt, blazer, suit all work. Refrain from too much of anything that would distract the Interviewer, including perfume, makeup, or clothes that are too small, too big, or require constant adjusting.

TRY TO RELAX- and be yourself during your Interview. You can do this by being prepared to discuss who you are and your interests. Don't be surprised if the Interviewer takes notes, as they will most likely need to provide a write-up about you to their school. Be prepared for open-ended questions like. "Tell me a little bit about yourself." Before your interview, jot down bullet points you would like to mention so you can easily talk about yourself. This could be about your academic interests, athletics, extracurriculars, community service, internships, or essential work you have done. You may be asked what your favorite (class, book, movie, city, subject, teacher, etc.) is. Be prepared to answer why something is your favorite.

PREPARE- Identify two or three questions to ask the Interviewer - something that cannot be found on the website or marketing materials - e.g., favorite thing to do on campus, favorite professor, class, best memory. This allows the Interviewer to talk about their school.

Some things the Interviewer will be trying to figure out about you are: What excites you about school, life, and the future? Can you express your interest in the world, whether in politics or the environment? What are your passions? Have you explored them in-depth? Do you demonstrate intellectual curiosity? Are you easy to talk with, a diamond in the rough, sincere, articulate, etc.? Are you someone they would want for their child's roommate? The Interviewer is looking for people who will do well at their school. They may ask you if you have done any research or worked on something that involved original thinking. Think about something you might have done that was significant to you and why. Have you placed or received any honors or awards locally, regionally, or nationally? Bring something that demonstrates your strengths or interest, e.g., if you worked on the school newspaper and have an article you are proud of or is well written. It could be a piece of art or slides. If you have a resume, bring it to share.

What kind of community service have you done? If you haven't done community service, explain why not or what you have been doing, e.g., working, internship, sports, taking care of family members, etc. Interviewers are more interested in local community service vs. "the international trip." Did you have an internship? What did you do? What did you learn?

Have you faced adversities that impacted what you might have been able to do? If you feel comfortable sharing, you may want to talk about how you responded to them and the positive steps you took.

The Interviewer will have basic details about you, but probably not much. For example, they will likely not know your GPA, classes, etc.

Remember at the end of the Interview to stand up, thank them, and shake their hand. Also, ask if you can email or contact them if you have further questions. Even though you may already have their contact information, ask again.

Send a thank-you note a day or two later, either by email or snail mail.

....

"to ED or not to ED"

The first wave of application deadlines, REA (Restricted Early Action - non-binding), EA (Early Action - non-binding), and ED (Early Decision - binding), is just around the corner. Students that have had the time and support, and are good planners, may be taking advantage of these application options. For some students, completing the college application phase early allows them to settle into their senior year without feeling entrenched in essays and application details. In addition, there is always the incentive to find out early where they will attend. Gauging whether to apply early can be a good application plan but requires answering several questions beyond stating, "If accepted, I will attend!" In addition to creating the right application timeline, spotting the meaning in messages that colleges send out like: "we offer holistic reviews," "apply broadly to our school," or "there is no difference between EA, ED, or RD" and (wink, wink) "everyone will have a fair shot," is part of doing your homework. Specifically, try to answer what percentage of the admitted class is accepted during EA, ED, EDII, and RD. Look at the ED vs. RD rate. Can you figure out if a school's application options are about moving up the U.S. News Rankings? Is part of your application strategy geared towards getting into a highly selective school or a program like Engineering or Computer Science? Deciding to apply to ED also requires understanding whom ED favors, that there are more qualified students applying than spots available, and digesting the reality that a strong GPA, excellent test scores, and stellar extracurriculars will not necessarily be enough to be admitted.

While the *relevance of standardized test scores continues to be debated, for many highly selective schools, test scores are still a factor. For schools that receive many applications, test scores are one data point to help quickly sift applications into piles. Have you done a reality check on where your test scores fit with the scores for admitted students? Add this to your assessment equation.

You will also need to be aware of the potential changes in admissions prompted by the Department of Justice and the National Association for College Admission Counseling rule changes.[5] While the impact of those changes on students is still evolving, once again, the winds of admissions

---

5   Korn, Melissa, and Anne Tergesen. "College Admissions Group Votes to Allow More Aggressive Student Recruiting." Wall Street Journal, 28 September 2019

are shifting. Whether colleges will increase their deposit amounts, offer incentives for housing options, financial discounts, etc., or if the May 1st deadline becomes more fluid are purely speculative but ones that continue to float in the news. This does not mean that students should now adjust their application plans based on speculation. Instead, they can take advantage of the time leading up to submitting their applications to weigh out if ED is the right path for them. Seniors should complete and submit their applications based on the work they have done to determine their best college fits and well-thought-through application plans.

As you prepare to submit your applications, you may want to incorporate some of these questions to help you determine "to ED or not to ED." Be sure to add your own questions.

- What factors do you need to know when applying to schools that may be in your Reach category or have an admit rate of 25% or lower?

- Have you identified if a school is a "Likely," "Best Fit," or "Reach" yet?

- Have you visited the school you're considering applying to ED?

- Do you have a list of "Whys" that line up with what makes a particular school ED worthy (e.g., majors, costs, extracurriculars, location, size, campus culture, etc.)?

- Has the school increased or decreased admitted student classes? Some schools like George Washington have pared back their admitted classes, while others like Santa Clara aim to increase their enrollment, but in particular programs.

- What are the school's mission priorities, and how does it impact early admission options- e.g., public universities with guidelines and percentages?

- How many Out-of-State or In-State students do they accept?

- Can you afford to attend with or without Financial Aid?

- Are you excited and ready to go to college - without second thoughts?

- Are your parents ready for you to go to college - without second thoughts?

For the highly qualified student with an eye on a highly selective school, deciding to apply Early Decision is about more than finding a single dream school. Instead, applying Early Decision requires committed research to assess if a school is a true match, grounded with accessible information. What many students and families don't realize is that the majority of students apply for Regular Decision, and grappling with the Early Decision quandary is not a necessity of the college application journey. Instead, it is a choice of "to ED or not to ED."

*With many more schools moving to test-optional, be sure to check what the current policy is and will be to assess where scores fit.

....

the student-athlete
- jumping through hoops

While the number of opportunities to play sports in colleges diminishes significantly (see NCAA graphic), that doesn't mean a student can't continue to pursue athletics as part of their college experience. Navigating the athletic process is more than registering with the NCAA and meeting the GPA requirements. For the high school athlete, looking for the right college division, team, and program demands almost as much attention as their academic search, layering an intricate and complex amount of information to wade through. Including other essential college priorities that specifically identify costs, scholarships, eligibility, team culture, and academic offerings will be necessary to a college search. Using the guiding principle "choose the school, not the team" will help ensure a successful college strategy and a backup plan in case of injury, coach departure, academic struggles, or interest changes. The dream of playing a sport in college is often built on years of hard work, dedication, and sacrificing participating in other activities.

With that in mind, finding schools that provide the strongest educational opportunities for athletes, balance time commitments and travel, and are financially affordable is critical to pursuing athletics - at any level: DI, II, III, or intramural. With time and effort, athletics don't have to end in high school; for the student that thrives on the mind-body balance that a sport provides, it is one area in the college search that should not be overlooked.

Estimated Probability of Competing in College Athletics

	High School Participants	NCAA Participants	Overall % HS to NCAA	% HS to NCAA Division I	% HS to NCAA Division II	% HS to NCAA Division III
Men						
Baseball	482,740	36,011	7.5%	2.2%	2.3%	2.9%
Basketball	540,769	18,816	3.5%	1.0%	1.0%	1.4%
Cross Country	269,295	14,303	5.3%	1.8%	1.4%	2.1%
Football	1,006,013	73,712	7.3%	2.9%	1.9%	2.5%
Golf	143,200	8,485	5.9%	2.0%	1.6%	2.2%
Ice Hockey	35,283	4,323	12.3%	4.8%	0.6%	6.8%
Lacrosse	113,702	14,603	12.8%	3.1%	2.5%	7.3%
Soccer	459,077	25,499	5.6%	1.3%	1.5%	2.7%
Swimming	136,638	9,799	7.2%	2.8%	1.2%	3.2%
Tennis	159,314	7,785	4.9%	1.6%	1.0%	2.3%
Track & Field	605,354	28,914	4.8%	1.9%	1.2%	1.7%
Volleyball	63,563	2,355	3.7%	0.7%	0.7%	2.3%
Water Polo	22,475	1,072	4.8%	2.7%	0.8%	1.3%
Wrestling	247,441	7,300	3.0%	1.0%	0.8%	1.2%
Women						
Basketball	399,067	16,509	4.1%	1.3%	1.2%	1.7%
Cross Country	219,345	15,624	7.1%	2.7%	1.7%	2.7%
Field Hockey	60,824	6,119	10.1%	2.9%	1.4%	5.8%
Golf	79,821	5,436	6.8%	2.8%	1.9%	2.1%
Ice Hockey	9,650	2,531	26.2%	8.9%	1.1%	16.2%
Lacrosse	99,750	12,452	12.5%	3.7%	2.6%	6.2%
Soccer	394,105	28,310	7.2%	2.4%	1.9%	2.9%
Softball	362,038	20,419	5.6%	1.8%	1.7%	2.2%
Swimming	173,088	12,980	7.5%	3.3%	1.2%	3.0%
Tennis	189,436	8,596	4.5%	1.5%	1.0%	2.0%
Track & Field	488,267	30,326	6.2%	2.8%	1.5%	1.9%
Volleyball	452,808	17,780	3.9%	1.2%	1.1%	1.6%
Water Polo	21,735	1,217	5.6%	3.3%	1.1%	1.2%

Sources: High school figures from the 2018-19 High School Athletics Participation Survey conducted by the National Federation of State High School Associations; data from club teams not included. College numbers from the NCAA 2018-19 Sports Sponsorship and Participation Rates Report.

Last Updated: April 8, 2020

- Colleges receive more applications when their basketball teams do well.[6]
- Why Sports and Elite Academics Do Not Mix[7]
- How College Sports Killed Summer Vacation[8]
- Want to Play College Sports? Here are Your Best Chances.[9]

---

6 Pope, Devin, and Jaren Pope. "Colleges receive more applications when their basketball teams do well." Economist, 2018
7 Cole, Jonathan R. "Why Sports and Elite Academics Do Not Mix." The Atlantic, 2017
8 Tracy, Marc. "How College Sports Killed Summer Vacation." The New York Times, 31 July 2018
9 Curran, David. "Want to play college sports? Here are your best chances." SFGATE, 19 November 2017

calculating college costs
& completing FAFSA®

Whether your family has been building a nest egg or a 529 account, the cost of attending college is expensive. Becoming familiar with the terminology of "College Financial Aid" and utilizing tools like the Federal Student Aid Estimator[10] can make estimating college costs easier, clarify if you qualify for need-based financial aid, and help prioritize which colleges should be on your college list. Understanding financial aid terminology and utilizing tools like the Net Price Calculator, which can be found on each college's website, will help you find answers to your financial need questions and help you assess if an Early Decision application path is viable and the right plan for you. It will also help prepare you for the FAFSA® process,[11] which typically opens on October 1st.

Look for updates on when the FAFSA® form will be available and check out these additional resources:

- Access the FAFSA® form at fafsa.gov.

- How FAFSA Simplification Will Change Financial Aid Eligibility[12]

- 8 Steps to Completing the FAFSA® form.[13]

- The CSS Profile (College Scholarship Service Profile).[14] Used for Merit Aid.

- FAFSA® Application Deadlines [15]

- Understanding the FAFSA® Process for Parents[16]

....

10 "Federal Student Aid Estimator." Federal Student Aid
11 "FAFSA® Application." Federal Student Aid
12 Kantrowitz, Mark. "How FAFSA® Simplification Will Change Financial Aid Eligibility." Saving for College
13 "8 Steps to Completing the FAFSA® Form – Federal Student Aid." Federal Student Aid
14 CSS Profile – CSS Profile
15 "FAFSA® Application Deadlines." Federal Student Aid
16 "Understanding the FAFSA® Process for Parents – Federal Student Aid." Federal Student Aid

1. Will I qualify for financial aid—either need-based[1] or merit aid?

2. What is the difference between need-based and merit aid?

3. Can merit aid bring the cost to attend college closer to what I will pay at a public university in my home state? Which schools will be likely to give me merit aid?

4. What is EFC (Expected Family Contribution),[2] and how can I find out https://studentaid.gov/aid-estimator/what mine will be? Note. This changed in 2023, to the Student Aid Index (SAI).[3]

5. What documents[4] will I need to start filling out the FAFSA® form?

6. How do I fill out the FAFSA® form?[5]

7. What is the difference between FAFSA® and CSS?[6]

8. Do I need to fill out the FAFSA® and CSS for all schools on my college list?

9. Does your state require you to complete the FAFSA®?[7]

10. How do I renew my FAFSA® Application?[8]

---

1 Helhoski, Anna, and Des Toups. "What is Need-Based Financial Aid?" NerdWallet, 15 June 2022

2 "What is my Expected Family Contribution (EFC)?" Federal Student Aid

3 Tretina, Kat. "What Is The Student Aid Index? – Forbes Advisor." Forbes, 21 April 2021,

4 "Filling Out the FAFSA® Form." Federal Student Aid

5 "Filling Out the FAFSA® Form." Federal Student Aid

6 Barnes, Erin. "FAFSA & CSS Profile - A Straightforward Guide to Understanding Financial Aid." Scoir

7 Carrns, Ann. "More States Require High School Seniors to Fill Out Financial Aid Form." The New York Times, 14 October 2022,

8 "How to Renew Your FAFSA® Application." Federal Student Aid,

"The good life is a process,

not a state of being.

It is a direction, not a destination."

-Carl Rogers

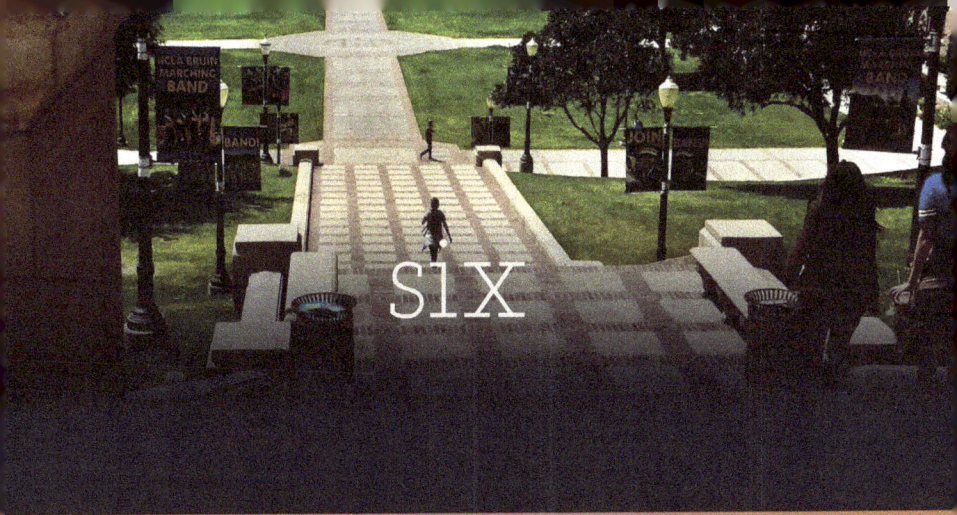

SIX

pie, pivoting, pass on the college talk
-surviving the holidays.

Celebration, relief, re-grouping, and resilience may all in come into play for seniors and families as admissions decisions are released. Holidays can be particularly tricky for seniors caught between finals and finishing up college applications and trying to catch their breath, looking forward to their school break and gathering with family. Planning for what to say when Aunt Gertrude corners them, between her polite requests to pass the stuffing, with "Have you gotten accepted yet?" and "What will you major in?" can smooth out holiday celebrations and Christine Koubek's Washington Post article, "Tired of people asking where you're going to college? Here's what to say."[1] gives some guidance as families bundle off to Grandma's house (or not), break bread, and give thanks. Learn to pivot conversations— Think about what you want to say and what you don't want to say before family gatherings. The moment to share good news will come sooner than everyone realizes, so it's o.k. not to have every conversation be about college.

1. Ask Aunt Gertrude a question. Your college process may be reminding her of her days in college. Let her share the good stuff. Where did you go to college? What did you like about it?

---

1 Koubek, Christine. "Tired of people asking where you're going to college? Here's what to say." The Washington Post, 23 February 2017

2. Change the subject. Talk about pie, the best way to cook a turkey, or which football team you think may win.

3. Rally the troops. While you are more than capable of shifting a conversation, engage your best allies – your parents. Ask them to be ready to help deflect questions.

✓ Navigating the convergence of holiday gatherings and college application season with a little pre-meal planning can be as easy as - well, pie.
Need a few more tips? Keep reading.

• Protecting Friendships During the College Admissions Process,[1] Susannah L. Griffe "While You're Waiting" [2]Meghan Mchale Dangremond Tufts Blog

For seniors finishing up their final applications and supplemental essays (keep going!), here are empowering tips that offer practical guidance on how to prepare for the next phase and remind students that their path to college doesn't only point to one school.

• Tip Sheet: If You Are Accepted, Rejected or Deferred[3] NY Times, Tanya Abrams

• A Dean's Advice to Seniors: Don't Slack Off[4] Martha C. Merrill

• 6 Tips About College Admissions Results[5], Tanya Caldwell

1 Griffe, Susannah L. "Protecting Friendships During the College Admissions Process." New York Times, 5 December 2011
2 Mchale Dangremond, Meghan. "While You're Waiting." Tufts Blog
3 Abrams, Tanya. "Tip Sheet: If You Are Accepted, Rejected or Deferred." New York Times, 27 March 2013
4 Merrill, Martha C. "A Dean's Advice to Seniors: Don't Slack Off." New York Times, 6 February 2012
5 Caldwell, Tanya. "6 Tips About College Admissions Results - The New York Times." The New York Times Web Archive, 30 March 2012

second-semester senior
- don't catch senioritis

As a senior, you are now officially in the waiting-for-decisions period and starting the homestretch of senior year. While you may feel ready to take your foot off the gas, you should think about finding a good cruising speed that allows you to:

1. Continue to do well in classes and avoid lower grades that could impact your acceptances or scholarships.

2. Take the time to write Thank You letters to teachers, counselors, and others who wrote a recommendation letter on your behalf. The people who have championed you in high school will be rooting for you long after graduation, and you never know if you may want to ask them again to write another letter for an internship or job or serve as a personal reference.

3. Keep doing the things that make you happy!!!

4. If you have multiple acceptances, start weighing the pros and cons to help you determine which schools are your strongest fits. Make sure to include the cost to attend (tuition, books, room/board, student fees, and transportation), the academic program, will AP credits be accepted, the distance between school and home, and anything else important for your successful leap to college.

5. If you have already decided on which school to attend, send in a Housing Deposit to start securing Housing early. Send your deposit and SIR (Statement of Intent to Register) to the school you plan to attend next fall and tell all schools that have offered you acceptance that you will not attend.

6. By now, many Early Action notifications, schools with rolling decisions, and some CSUs have released their admission notifications. Remember to stay on top of your email and portals in case one of your schools needs something from you, like, mid-term grades or test scores.

The majority of admission decisions will come out in March. So, while you are in "waiting mode," here are a few more tips from Tufts admissions' blog, called "While You're Waiting,"[2] to help keep you focused, be present, and enjoy senior year with only the slightest hints of senioritis!

One statement I often hear from second-semester seniors is, "phew, I can finally relax." Enjoying senior year as you get ready to graduate is part of your journey to college. Knowing expectations from colleges you've been admitted into is also part of your journey to college and will help you continue to strike the right balance between academics, extracurricular activities, and downtime. This blog post, "How to stay admitted,"[3] from Jeff Schiffman, former Director of Admission at Tulane, will help clarify what colleges expect.

Stumped on how to write a Thank You note? Here's "How Write a Great Thank You Letter"[4] will get you started.

....

decisions. decisions. decisions.

The admission decision season is here. Who wouldn't want to receive a new kitten or puppy to go with their decision notifications? For seniors, college admission decisions may come with banners, t-shirts, or thin envelopes. While receiving a welcome or consolation puppy in the mail is unlikely, the good news is that preparing for what to expect can help you respond, plan your next steps, and embrace news in a way that honors your unique educational journey and keeps you focused on your path to college. Outside of rolling admissions, college decisions will come in waves and continue until the end of March/early April. There is a good chance you will receive a mix of news in the coming weeks and months - acceptance, deferral, waitlist, or not accepted. Your expectations and support system can help you navigate this part to make decisions that continue to reflect your goals and aspirations. Hopefully, your college journey has included learning about the nature of college

2 Mchale Dangremond, Meghan. "While You're Waiting." Tufts Blog

3 Schiffman, Jeff. "How to Stay Admitted." Tulane University Admission Blog - Jeff Schiffman, 12 January 2021

4 Hertzberg, Karen. "How to Write the Perfect Thank You Letter." Grammarly, 13 May 2019

admissions and creating a balanced college list so that you can approach decision season with manageable expectations and goals.

Unfortunately, waiting for college admission news can be stressful. My advice: Stay in your lane. This is when it's essential to continue making decisions based on what is best for you. Commit yourself and focus on your vision of what you want in a college experience. Everyone else's news should be nothing more than white noise.

early decision notifications

If you have received an ED acceptance – congratulations, you're in and know where you're going to college. It also means you must withdraw all other applications you have submitted, send in your SIR (Statement of Intent to Register), and deposit. If you are moved into a Regular Decision path, while not the news you may have wanted to hear, you may be able to take advantage of an Early Decision II pathway. So, if you haven't added those deadlines in or completed those essays, it's time to polish them up and shift gears to keep your options open.

what to do if you receive a deferral or not-accepted?

I'm not going to sugar-coat this – it may sting or knock the wind out of you. Even though this may feel personal, try to remember that there is a broader context in play. Many decisions are about the numbers and the specific enrollment mission of that college. Simply stated, there are many more applicants than spots. Take a moment to catch your breath. Stay focused, shake it off like "water off a duck's back," and this will soon become a distant memory.

what can you do, and how to respond if you receive a deferral?

Schools are typically particular on what you must do if you have been deferred or moved into the Regular Decision pile. Please pay attention to what they want. If they want you to opt in, do it and do it quickly. You have nothing to lose by doing that, and you continue to keep your options open. If they want more information from you, don't wait. Submit what they need to review your application. Some schools offer the opportunity to switch from EA to EDII, which may be an option worth considering after a review of your overall list and notifications. Some schools don't want anything. Try to sit tight. It may be challenging, but sending loads of new information, letters or cookies won't convince them that your application should rise to the top. Sometimes a short, well-crafted letter or email of continued interest may make sense, depending on the school.

what to do if you've been waitlisted?

Again, listen to what schools require, and respond quickly. With the ability for students to apply to multiple schools, it has become less clear to colleges which students will actually enroll. In response to this shift, many schools try to manage enrollment and acceptances via the waitlist or deferral. Opt-in if given that choice. You have nothing to lose. While you're waiting, try to find out the statistics of students who get off the waitlist. Recognize that there is a considerable range in how schools address waitlists which may vary from year to year.

what to do if you have multiple acceptances?

Multiple acceptances are an excellent "problem." While it may feel a little daunting to think about choosing between colleges, making a decision will be based on weighing priorities, making choices, and analyzing tradeoffs. Keep in mind, however, that there will be no perfect school. If a school feels perfect to you, it is probably a good fit. Once you've received all of your notifications, you can review each school within an overall context, which will be different from your original college list. For some students, the best-fit school will rise out of the pile. Other students may need to sift through nuances, including cost, major, or distance from home. This is the time to pull in your counselor, parent, or trusted adult to help you walk through your priorities to determine your best fit school based on factual information, not speculation.

A considerable part of the college search is learning to make decisions, small and large, along the way. This involves building a list, deciding when to apply, and determining which application decision pool (RD, EA, ED) makes the most sense for you. These tasks help you build decision-making skills to respond to college decisions that are consistent with your priorities. The bonus is that you can take these decision-making skills with you wherever you choose to go.

- The Waitlist. Why?!,[5] Rick Clark, Georgia Tech Admissions

....

apples, kiwis, mangoes
- deciding where to attend

While it is often the case that deciding where to attend college is the culmination of the college search and application process, learning how to make that decision is also very much a part of the process. One method to help students with the decision phase is comparing "apples to apples" regarding potential college choices by re-visiting and prioritizing their initial college experience criteria. Remembering those critical aspects is often easy, but assigning value and importance to each particular criterion may be more challenging. The initial college application list may look uniform with consistent criteria that check all the boxes for each student, whether a preference for a large public university, a major metropolitan area, a research university, or a liberal arts school surrounded by rolling hills. Once acceptances are known, that list shifts. Where there once were 10-12 schools, now there may be three, five, or seven schools to choose from. It was not surprising when one of my students said their list looked more like apples, kiwis, and mangoes. To move forward and choose, students need to understand the specific nuances, i.e., whether and why a certain kind of apple, kiwi, or mango is best for them.

Whatever seeds of interest resulted in schools being on your college list, and now your acceptance list may have evolved since you first chose them. From the time applications are submitted to the time acceptances are received, students have grown, developed new interests, and potentially incorporated new ways of thinking that redefine what is essential to them.

---

5   Clark, Rick. "The Waitlist. Why?!" Georgia Tech Admission Blog, 23 March 2021

Revisiting the qualities and factors you want in your college experience and now deciding their relative importance can add clarity and help reveal the similarities and distinctions between colleges where you've been accepted. While you need to develop your own QUESTIONS, try answering some of these questions as a warmup:

- Does the school culture and environment support who you are?

- Are there clubs and organizations that fit your interests academically and socially or offer opportunities to explore?

- Could you envision yourself in late-night banter about esoteric topics or binging on Netflix with your roommates?

- Are you excited that campus and city are one and taking mass transit to classes, to the grocery store, or to travel home for breaks is just what you want?

- Did you learn that a well-regarded professor will teach courses in your major?

- Was a new 3-2 program introduced that fits with what you want to study?

- Is there a robust career placement center that will support finding internships and jobs?

- Is your financial package enough so that college will be affordable?

- Do you see yourself walking across campus with crisp leaves crunching under your feet and studying on the lawn of the main quad?

- Maybe it is none of these, and you found an internship in Iceland dug up months after applications were submitted.

- Did you attend *Admitted Students' Day, and the weather was slushy and grey, but the idea of throwing on one more layer of clothing and finding out what it's like to live in what people call "seasons" was the new bonus of a particular college? *Not all schools will host in-person Admitted Student Days, and some may be offered virtually to accommodate students.

- Do the students seem friendly or people you would hang out with? Do you need to attend a Student Ambassador Chat to find out?

What seniors come to learn is that choosing a college often involves trade-offs. The choices may be between warm weather or a school with a quarter system, or one school has extensive resources and libraries. In contrast, another has a small teacher-to-student ratio, or it may be based on which college offers a more robust financial package. The list of trade-offs could be endless but will be specific to the student. Prioritizing what will be the most important characteristics will help with making a decision.

For some seniors, deciding where to go to college will be easy and exciting. For others, it will be so monumentally important that indecision can capture them, even if cushioned in family support. There is no one perfect school. A student's strengths and accomplishments are embedded in who they are and will go with them no matter which college they choose. Remembering this can give students confidence that they are shaping their future and help reaffirm which school is their best fit as they decide which they prefer - apples, kiwis or mangoes.

....

ten tips to prepare for college May Day

As the May 1st date to submit your SIR (Statement of Intent to Register) and deposit to the college you will attend in the fall is just a few days away, I want to congratulate you.

Whether you're doing a victory dance or exhaling a long sigh of relief, your acceptance into college started with a dream, your #college dream. Along your college journey, you may have faced crossroads, made choices, and possibly seen that there are many pathways for your future. Yes, acceptance can be found in the joy an email or letter brings, but acceptance is an invitation to step into your life, make intentional decisions, and embrace your future. Going to college is just the beginning of your amazing life. You made this happen. You will continue to be in charge of your success. Congratulations! It's time to celebrate you. 🥳🎉

TIP ONE: Finish your school year strong - now is the time to avoid senioritis and low grades. Remember that your final transcript will be submitted to the college you're going to, AND your grades should align with your application.

TIP TWO: Check your emails from your school. Make sure you are on top of deadlines for housing, orientation, submitting documents, tuition payments, etc., and know what the fall semester will look like so you can plan for it.

TIP THREE: Sign-up for housing and send in your deposit. The early bird catches the worm and snags a dorm room.

TIP FOUR: Final transcripts need to be sent to your school in June. Your counselor may automatically do this, but you should check on this.

TIP FIVE: Call and email the Financial Aid office if you are working on any Financial Aid details or need to update because your family's financial situation has changed. Follow up on anything you need or what your college/office of financial assistance may need from you. Don't wait for your college to contact you. Financial Aid offices are there to walk you through your financial aid package and answer your questions. You are your own best advocate, so be sure to speak up.

TIP SIX: Attend Orientation - Your school's orientation program, whether on campus or virtual, will help you a) get acclimated, b) allow you to meet some of your newly accepted classmates, c) find out if you need to take any placement exams, d) are exempt from entry-level requirements, and e) possibly even pre-register for fall classes, depending on where you will be attending. If you can attend orientation, try to schedule as early as possible to work with your schedule. If the orientation is on campus and you can't travel, check if your college offers a local orientation program.

TIP SEVEN: Families/Parents may be offered their own orientation sessions on Financial Aid, Family Educational Rights and Privacy Act (FERPA) in College[1] and *Legal Documents you may

1   Dix, Willard. "You Need to Understand Your Educational Rights." Forbes, 2018

want,[*2] Health Insurance, Dorm Insurance, Tuition Insurance,[3] Academic or Disability Support, Wellness Programs, Parents' Weekends, and other school-specific programs.

TIP EIGHT: Send any AP scores that may qualify for credit at your school. If you are unsure about this, the College Board website has that information. Every school is different on what score will be considered for credit or allow you to place out of a course.

TIP NINE: Let your other accepted schools know that you will not be attending.

TIP TEN: Send Thank You notes. If you haven't sent a letter to teachers, counselors, coaches, or anyone else that has supported you during the college application process or throughout high school, now is the time - and share your good news with them. They will be happy to hear from you.

---

2 Leonard, Ben, et al. "Three Critical Legal Documents Every Parent of a College Student Should Get in Place As Soon As Possible." National Law Review, 26 September 2017

3 GradGuard | College Life Pro

BONUS TIP: If you're thinking about taking a Gap year or deferring enrollment, check your college's policy to understand what you are bound to and what is and is not possible. Some schools prohibit students from 1) enrolling in college courses (which can include community colleges or pre-college programs that offer college credit) or 2) applying to any other colleges, or 3) may not allow for Gap years, and you would need to reapply to their school if you choose not to attend. Know the parameters before changing your college plans and recognize that every college has its own policy.

what legal documents do your kids need before going to college?[6]

*Every family and student will have different needs and requirements. These suggestions reflect a starting place for families and are by no means exhaustive for what each student and family may need. It is the responsibility of each family to research and determine all documents that will be required for their college student.

---

6 Fletcher, Christine. "What Legal Documents Do Your Kids Need Before Going To College?" Forbes, 29 August 2018

inhale the future
- new school year, new opportunities.

As a soon-to-be first-year student may tell you – they've been primed for the "best years of their life" once they arrive on a college campus. Maybe their "senior summer" has been a mix of goodbyes and good times with friends and family. Breathing in the relief of knowing where they will be in the fall, yet realizing that it may feel a little like the first day of kindergarten, may require pulling out forgotten skills. A fresh start may be precisely what some first-year students need. So much of the college search focuses on finding the best-fit schools to build familiarity and opportunities. Putting into place skills that will help students engage as soon as they arrive at school will help first-year students settle into their new campus home and have a successful transition. Successful college experiences are about what you do while you're there. The polished image of college life may gloss over the steps a student may need to take to help build college success. The transition to college may require a little scaffolding.

Having guidance from Michelle Obama's Reach Higher- Better Make Room [7] A Student's Guide to Your First Year of College YouTube series,[8] the University of Michigan Survival Guide 101,[9] and books like "Your Turn,"[10] by Julie Lythcott-Haims, can help students prepare for move-in day, their first year at college, and help to smooth out some of the bumps and optimize the first-year college experience.

Try new things. Try new things. Try new things.

I'll say it again. Try new things.

....

7   Better Make Room: Home
8   "A Student's Guide To Your First Year of College." YouTube, 19 September 2019
9   "UMich 101: New Student Survival Guide - Office of Undergraduate Admissions."
University of Michigan Admission
10   Lythcott-Haims, Julie. Your Turn: How to Be an Adult. Henry Holt and Company, 2022.

PARTICIPATE: Raise your hand. Sit in front of your classes. Eat in the cafeteria. Talk to students and faculty in the elevator, the lobby, or in the halls. Look for friendly faces in classes - they could be part of your new study group.

ORIENTATION: Sign up for activities that will introduce you to your new campus, town, or classmates.

CLUBS: Ready to try something new? Sign up early in the semester. Try out one or two clubs or community service groups. Hesitant? Start with something easy like a Squirrel club. Figure out which clubs you like. Ask around for suggestions.

ACADEMIC SUPPORT: Find out if there is academic support on campus. What are the hours? How does it work? Are services capped? Do they need to be scheduled or on a first-come, first-served basis? Are services free? Will you need tools to help you stay on top of assignments and projects? Is it time for a bullet journal or a new app?

ATHLETICS: Were you an athlete in high school? Look for club and intramural teams that offer flexibility, but provide the challenge level and team spirit you're looking for. Try a new sport that you didn't have time for. Your interest and ability might be a great fit for something new. Go to sporting events. Some campuses with team sports offer discounted tickets for students.

WELLNESS: Catch a cold? Have a sore throat? Need someone to talk to? Rely on breaking a sweat to recharge or de-stress? Taking care of "you" is key to being a successful college student. Knowing what health services are available, the time of drop-in hours, and the pharmacy's location before you need them will help you handle any bumps. Take a recreational class or use the Rec Center. Nothing beats stress more than a good workout.

SHOW UP TO CLASSES: Why go to college if you're not going to attend class? Even if you're stuck with a few 8:00 a.m. classes, go to class. It may mean an earlier bedtime the night before, but the whole point of college is about learning. With each semester or quarter, you'll figure out how to nab a better schedule.

GO TO OFFICE HOURS: Face-to-face conversations with your professors can expand how you approach your classes and learning in general. Conversations with your professor may lead to finding out what brought them to love the subject they're teaching, and their career path and may even create opportunities for working in that field or help you refine what you want to major in.

"Whenever they say it can't be done, remind them that they make a jellybean that tastes exactly like popcorn."

-John Mayer

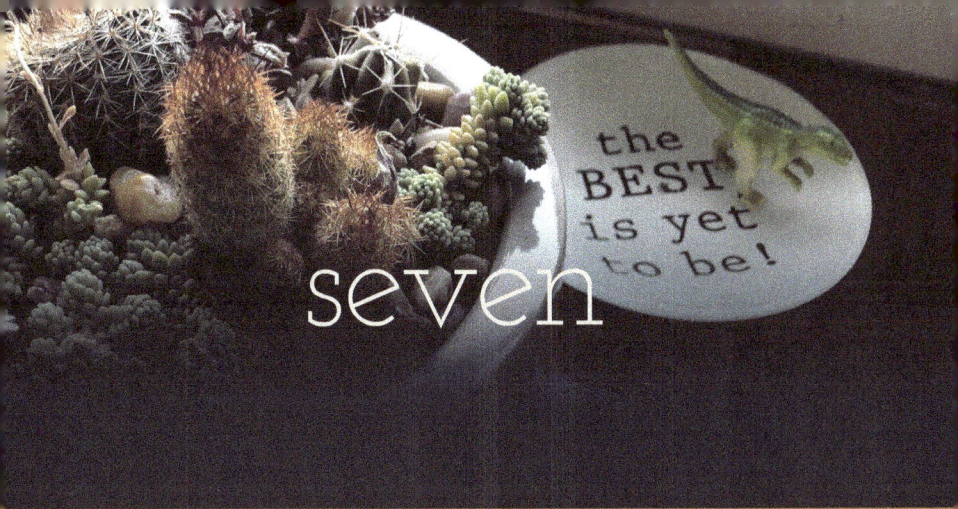

seven

HICCUPS

Twists and Hiccups

Torn ACL, failing grades, family health challenges, job loss, move to a new state or school, or pandemic are not usually part of what students and families aspire toward when thinking about their high school experience or college experience, but life in its "to -be-counted-on-for -unpredictability," happens. When hitting a bump in the road, running into an obstacle, or my favorite word, hiccup, time can often be the salve and solution. Sometimes, though, more is needed, which may include more support, e.g., tutoring, working with your high school teachers and counselors, medical support, a plan, e.g., revising course loads, activities (lightening or increasing), or a pause to regain balance and finding a new pace or stride. It's easy to think that life is lock-step, or if you do A, then B will follow. Sometimes the surprise that living comes with twists and turns and learning how to navigate those are more often the bigger part of the journey. In Susan Cain's book Bittersweet, she writes, "Bittersweet feelings create momentum for change and help us find our purpose because they point us toward inner truths about our lives and what matters most to us."[1] And embracing that duality of "the dark as well

---

1 Cain, Susan. Bittersweet: How Sorrow and Longing Make Us Whole. Crown, 2022. Should You Hire a College Consultant for Your Student?

as the light -- is, paradoxically, the only way to transcend them."[2] While this sentiment may not completely lessen the pain of a setback or resolve a hiccup, embracing it can help, coupled with patience and self-compassion, while rebuilding a revised trajectory forward. Growth does not always look tidy, and it may not come as a surprise that evolving young adults go through multiple evolutions, whether changing their minds multiple times about what to major in at college or what they value most. Adaptability that may include strategies and a new lens can be integral, but time will be critical for development and refinding their footing.

....

the crunch, crack, ouch of 2020 - don't panic.

It wasn't supposed to be this way. My running distance was ticking up without injury. I know I'll never be the fastest, but running has saved my soul too many times to skip a day. It didn't seem unreasonable to start planning a new goal, envisioning my future runs. With the pandemic, staying at home, and masking up, it seemed like the perfect time to challenge myself. That is precisely what I was telling my husband on a late summer hike, and then came the Crunch.

Gravel and weak ankles have been my opponents for years. With the number of twists my ankles have had, one might think I am part human and part Gumby. Ice packs and ace bandages are always on hand. I've learned the difference between the twists that will sideline me and those I can lightly push through. This made me think my new 2020 goal may be put on hold. The pace of our hike slowed as I reassessed the swelling and the pain, preparing myself for what the impacts would be. That was Sunday. I plopped down on the couch on Monday, beating the sunrise with coffee and ready to get to work. The quiet would soon be complemented by tapping the keyboard. I leaned left to grab my laptop - a simple enough task even without the caffeine kick. As I reached toward the side table, my body slipped and fell into the arm of the couch. Crack.

2   Suttie, Jill. "How Sorrow and Longing Enrich Your Life." Greater Good Science Center, 17 May 2022, https://greatergood.berkeley.edu/article/item/how_sorrow_and_longing_enrich_your_life.

It was a "What the heck?" moment as I heard my ribs crunch and felt a wave of unfamiliar pain. I want to say I yelped, "Ouch," but I guess it was more guttural. My next thought was, "Don't Panic." Activities like running, which I love and seem integral to managing and adapting to 2020, appeared in jeopardy at that moment.

This personal story is no different from most high school students' experiences in switching to Staying at Home, distance learning, pass/ no pass grading, canceled standardized tests, and virtual APs. I will stop here because you know the picture -- you lived it, after all. With all the changes in 2020, the path to college may have felt like it lurched into unknown territory. And yes, additional flexibility and patience were required, and reading the tea leaves probably seemed murky even for families who had been through the college journey before.

There was much focus on the high school class of 2020 and the significant adjustments and impacts that jolted them from the traditions they wanted to experience. However, they weren't alone, and the classes of 2021, 2022, 2023 and even 2024 participated in what was more than growing pains as they were sidelined and were forced to adapt to shifts and continually adjust schedules in classroom learning, applying to colleges, expectations, and social life. Many of the shifts stemmed from a desire to support students -- from sports practice being called on or off moving to virtual pods or a chalked circles to colleges adjusting

> **?** While questions like the ones below plagued students and families in 2020, some of those same questions still bubble up every application season.
>
> - How will my application be reviewed without a test score?
> - How many schools should I apply to?
> - Is it true that more students from the prior class will take up spots for the next class?
> - Will I be able to be on campus, and if so, will I be confined to my dorm?
> - What does "grace" mean during the application process, e.g., more application flexibility, delayed deadlines, and more supplemental essays to write?

expectations, deadlines, and test and essay requirements. It may have felt like everyone was making things up as we went along. Maybe. While I saw flexibility in the world, I also saw students experience a continual stream of unknowns with limited tools for interpreting what they heard while navigating their path to college.

For some students, 2020 shed light on clarifying what they wanted and what was important to them and helped them prioritize and learn how to advocate for themselves when being pulled along by external structures or when the activities that once gave their lives structure have dissipated. If ever a group of students felt "crunch," "crack," and "ouch," it has been the students moving from high school to college as caught in the temporary and long-term shifts of applying to college.

What remained and remains the same is the importance of striking a balance between adhering to the engaging things that provide happiness while figuring out how to move beyond a comfort zone. When the message drumming in everyone's ear was to stay at home felt more than challenging, and distance learning and online experiences were far from perfect, opportunities arose in the unknown and offered something that some students may not have tried in ordinary times. This is not a call to do more, like early pandemic mentions of Shakespeare writing King Lear during the plague (yes, I'm guilty here -- I did mention it). It's time to notice that there is often a chance for newfound intentionality despite setbacks or limitations. That may look like this:

- Digging into classes in or outside of school. Balanced course load and rigor = success.

- Volunteering virtually. Plowing through a stack of books hiding in the corner of your room. Writing the first draft of a novel (just because NANOWRIMO[3] has come and gone doesn't mean your ideas have gone, Poof!).

- Starting to plan your upcoming summer with a plan A (in-person) and plan B (virtual)

Recognizing that the crunch, crack, and ouch of 2020 was temporary and required patience and motivation - (for me, a new running playlist helped.) Taking advantage of the 10-10-10 rule to see ten months out, whether

---

3 NaNoWriMo: Welcome

planning or anticipating what may be right around the corner, can help students envision what their future may look like and also interpret what any shifts mean when applying to college. Framing this historical time as still evolving even as we look back and evaluate the impacts on higher education and what changed may include contextualizing admission adaptation, being aware that college-specific essays and test-optional policies are here to stay, and realizing a student's strengths and abilities are more than a standardized test score and developing a test plan may be different for each student. It's always a time to review what works and what doesn't. If goals or objectives need tweaking? Do students need to look beyond their backyards, back fences, and computer screens to retool or reinvent themselves into a renewed version of themselves? While glacially slow and painful, the crunch, crack, and ouch of 2020 did not mean students put off looking toward the future and making plans that ultimately led them to their college destination. While the future and the college path have often felt certain and lock-step, there has always been room to craft an individualized journey. And in so many ways, 2020 provided a refined lens to reflect and build on that knowledge. While our call to action in 2020 was to sit on the couch, a renewed perspective may heal the crunch, crack, and ouch we've all been through.

Life interruptus and planning for the future

I've been thinking about one of my favorite movies lately, Ben Stiller's version of "The Secret Life of Walter Mitty,"[4] based on James Thurber's 1939 short essay.[5] I keep returning to this movie for reasons beyond the soundtrack and the visual escapism that transports me to Greenland (fun fact: it was filmed in Iceland), which may be my version of managing a "stay-cation." What keeps pulling me to watch it is the underlying optimistic message that life is not linear and the affirmation that a life interrupted does not translate to a dead-end. While some folks may see Stiller's movie and Thurber's essay as about distractions or daydreams, I cannot help but see imagination, optimism, and possibility. These ideas

---

4   Stiller, Ben. "The Secret Life Of Walter Mitty - Trailer #1." YouTube, 31 July 2013

5   Thurber, James. "The Secret Life of Walter Mitty." The New Yorker, 1939

become more important as I take in the recent daily news and its impact on higher and secondary education and students.

I could be watching movies offering a more dystopian vision of what the future holds, but I prefer to look for ways to respond proactively, whether that may require developing skills for more meaningful and productive online experiences or creating more internal (rather than external) rhythms to guide my days and work. I am also eager to support students as they learn new skills, new ways to approach the world, and new routines, all without giving up their dreams and optimism, which may include recognizing what is temporary and what may be an opportunity hidden in the unexpected. Reading the article from Rick Clark, "Change is the Only Constant,"[6] is another helpful reminder that there is something new in college admissions every year. Scandals, waitlists, schools adding Early Decision II deadlines, FAFSA introducing new timing, and IRS retrieval tools are just a few reminders that what we think are sure things in college admissions may not always be the case. What we can rely on is our ability to stay nimble and informed.

Additionally, developing reasonable expectations about what a college means when they switch to test-optional and whom that applies to, or what an admit rate is and how that applies to individual students (e.g., athletes, legacies, first-gen, tuba players, or state-resident) will be important in the upcoming application cycles. This also means that students must seek colleges with programs, courses, and environments that support their aspirations and interests. It is hard to predict precisely what each upcoming admission cycle will look like.

It may be reasonable to expect that with major shifts for standardized testing and colleges incorporating online learning, the upcoming year may look different, and the return to what has felt like normal expectations and traditions may be delayed. Still, every day involves looking towards the future, whether for the upcoming ten minutes, hours, days, months, or years. Right now, it's too early to predict what summer or fall will be like, but this is an excellent time to explore alternative summer plans. Whether that means looking for online or local experiences, it is important to pay attention to how colleges are responding to current and future students and reaffirm your aspirations while knowing that many roads will lead to fulfilling them

---

6 Clark, Rick. "Change is the Only Constant." Georgia Tech Admission Blog, 20 March 2020

gap years
- who says the path is linear?

Many colleges offer gap year programs. Be sure to research options when applying to school. Find out which schools will honor a gap year and the requirements.

• Gap Year Deferral Policies for some colleges,[7] Gap Year Association

gap year programs to explore

• The Gap Year Association[8]

• Global Citizen Year[9]

• TeenLife.com[10]

• AmeriCorps[11]

• Where There Be Dragons[12]

• Youth Conservation Corp[13]

• Amigos International[14]

• Bay Area Youth Agency[15]

---

7   Gap Year Association
8   Gap Year Association
9   Global Citizen Year: Global Gap Year Program
10 TeenLife | Experiential Learning
11 "Answer the Call to Serve." AmeriCorps, 4 November 2020
12 "Gap Year Programs | Africa, Asia, America, Nepal, China | Dragons." Where There Be Dragons
13 Youth Conservation Corps (YCC): A YouthBuild Program in Lake County, IL
14 Volunteer Abroad for Teens in Latin America - AMIGOS
15 Bay Area Youth Agency

college gap year programs

- Colorado College[16]

- Brown University[17]

- Dartmouth[18]

- Tufts 1+4[19]

- Princeton[20]

gap year articles

- Gap Year? Do It Here William Deresiewicz, New York Times[21]

- Wondering What To Do In A Gap Year? Here's How To Spend It,[22] Ilana Hamilton

- Thinking About Taking A Gap Year Due To COVID-19? Here's How To Make The Most Of It:[23] Christopher Rim, Forbes

- Readers Tell Us: Is a Gap Year Worth it?[24] Sona Patel, New York Times

16   "The Gap Year Experience." Colorado College

17   "Additional Gap Year Resources | Curricular Resource Center." Brown University,

18   "Gap Year." Dartmouth Admissions

19   "Tufts Civic Semester | Tufts Admissions." Tufts University /

20   "Novogratz Bridge Year Program | Office of International Programs." Princeton OIP =

21   Deresiewicz, William. "Opinion | A Gap Year During the Coronavirus? Do It Here." The New York Times, 7 May 2020

22   Hamilton, Ilana. "How To Spend A Gap Year – Forbes Advisor." Forbes, 16 February 2023,

23   Rim, Christopher. "thinking-about-taking-a-gap-year-due-to-covid-19-here's-how-to-make-the-most-of-it" Forbes, 20 May 2020

24   Patel, Sona. "Readers Tell Us: Is a Gap Year Worth It? (Published 2017)." The New York Times, 6 April 2017

- How Taking a Gap Year Can Shape Your Life,[25] Ron Lieber, New York Times

- Why Harvard 'encourages' students to take a gap year. Just like Malia Obama is doing.[26] Valerie Strauss, Washington Post

- How to Plan a Gap Year [27] Shivani Vora, New York Times

- The Best Freshman Year is a Gap Year,[28] Abigail Falik and Linda Frey

25 Lieber, Ron. "How Taking a Gap Year Can Shape Your Life (Published 2016)." The New York Times, 19 October 2016

26 Strauss, Valerie, and Valerie Strauss. "Why Harvard 'encourages' students to take a gap year. Just like Malia Obama is doing." The Washington Post, 1 May 2016, /

27 Vora, Shivani. "How to Plan a Gap Year." The New York Times, 2 May 2016,

28 Falik, Abigail, and Linda Frey. "The Best Freshman Year is a Gap Year." The Chronicle of Higher Education

"Every great dream begins with a dreamer."

- Harriet Tubman

eight

TIPS & RESOURCES FOR PARENTS

support your teen
through their college search

Parents of seniors know their kids are working hard fall semester, not only in school but in providing answers in their applications to help schools understand who they are, what is essential to them for their college experience, and why they would be the best applicant to accept. Completing applications, writing essays, crossing the Ts, and dotting the I's require pacing and balancing priorities, as it can feel more like a marathon than a sprint. It's important to remember that your senior has a college list and goals that are unique to their aspirations and strengths, and "staying in their lane" will help them maintain the focus needed to achieve their goals. The fall is task-driven, and a good dose of levity, support, and assurances will improve this time for everyone. While it may seem counterintuitive, this is also a time when parents begin to step back and shift into supporting the independence needed to manage all things college successfully. Think of it as practice for the launch. Even as parents put on the observer or cheerleader hat during the application process, there are many ways parents can still help their teens during their college journey.

Limiting "college talk" to mutually agreed upon times within the week is one concrete strategy that allows seniors the time and opportunity to accomplish tasks independently and communicate with you when needing more support. Help your senior learn to pivot away from the onslaught of well-intentioned questions about their college search and application process. For friends, neighbors, and relatives, the entry point for a conversation with any junior or senior is often about school and college. While those chats can start in a good place, they can quickly move into talk of "a dream school," "top schools," and "how hard it is to get into college these days," all of which can become awkward and uncomfortable. Sometimes, changing the subject or asking a question may help shift the conversation to something everyone wants to discuss. Looking for more ideas on how to pivot? This Washington Post article is packed with advice and ideas on what a "pivot" can entail.

Getting ready to launch is not limited to preparation for the dorm drop-off. It can also include what you have to look forward to and what you need to know right now. Just as seniors need to stay in their lane during the application season, it's equally important for parents to see the road ahead and how to navigate the stretch they are headed toward. Try these six tips to help the college application and senior year go well. Got A Senior In High School? 6 Smart Ideas for Parenting Senior Year. The college search and application process is an optimal time for parents and teens to re-shift who's in charge and let teens practice ownership of responsibilities while still having a safety net in place. By taking the lead on this shift, parents can instill confidence in their teen's ability to be college-ready.

What else can parents do to support their teens through the college application season? Help send test scores. Make reservations for any last-minute college visits or spring decision visits. Be ready to fill out the Free Application for Federal Student Aid FAFSA and College Scholarship Profile CSS Profile, which opens October 1st.

....

navigating the college search

There is no doubt that a college education is a significant investment for both students and families and just like most investments,

Gather financial documents and read the articles below to help you be prepared.

- 8 Easy Steps for Parents Completing the FAFSA Form.
- What is the Student Aid Index?
- 7 Things You Need Before Filling Out the 2021-22 FAFSA® Form FAFSA's Expected Family Contribution Is Going Away. Good Riddance.

Have a junior in high school who is just getting started with building a college list, doing research, or planning college visits? These articles will help you establish a balanced perspective on what to expect.

- The Right Way to Choose a College, Dr. Denise Pope[1]
- Ask What Matters, Not Where Mary Hofstedt[2]
- Six Ways to Work With Your College Counselor, Willard Dix[3]
- Three Fears About Applying to College and How to Address Them Thomas Golden, Ph.D.[4]
- What I Wish I Knew During the College Search Process, Day-Tripper University[5]

---

1 Pope, Denise. "The Right Way to Choose a College." The Wall Street Journal, 22 March 2019

2 Hofstedt, Mary. "Ask What Matters, Not Where." Challenge Success, 2 March 2018

3 Dix, Willard. "Six Ways to Work With Your College Counselor." Forbes Magazine, 23 April 2018

4 Golden Ph. D., Thomas. "Three Fears About Applying To College and How To Address Them." Challenge Success, 13 September 2019,

5 Altman, Casey. "What I Wish I Knew During the College Search Process — Daytripper University." Daytripper University, 4 June 2019,

robust research and effort can enhance the outcome. Many families question whether my child can successfully navigate their college search and application process alone or if they will need more support and what kind of support. An IEC, or "college counselor," provides tools, resources, and assistance to help students build a personalized list of schools that are a strong personal match and fosters academic and social growth. The personalized attention, firsthand knowledge of hundreds of educational opportunities, and extensive experience with the college search and application process that an IEC (college counselor) provides enable students to explore options tailored to their needs, creating a positive and transformative decision-making experience.

"hiring a consultant can increase the odds of a good match. And parents avoid the year's worth of lost credits that don't transfer and the retaking of courses at the new school, which can add up and become costly"

. *Mark Sklarow, CEO of IECA*

Trying to decide what you need for a successful process? Tulane's former Admission Director, Jeff Schiffman, in his article, "So You're Using a College Counselor...,"[1] will help. The flood of information about the college search process often increases needless stress and competitive pressure. As a college counselor, I know it just doesn't have to be that way. While the unknown can be daunting to students and families, an IEC can help students engage in the college search with clear and strategic goals and realistic expectations. An IECs' experience and knowledge of both schools and the process broadens and helps refine a student's choices. By weighing the key factors such as academics, location, school culture, activities, and cost, an IEC can maximize student opportunities as they embark on the next steps in their education.

The articles below help weigh out the pros and cons in determining what support you may need and want, whether working with a high school college counselor, an independent college counselor, or managing your college search independently.

•   How to Find Trustworthy College Admissions Advice[2]

•   Should You Hire a College Consultant for Your Student?[3]

---

1   Schiffman, Jeff. "So You're Using a College Counselor." Tulane University Admission Blog, 11 January 2019

2   Halpert, Julie. "How to Find Trustworthy College Admissions Advice." The New York Times, 18 March 2019, https://www.nytimes.com/2019/03/18/well/family/college-bribery-scandal-admissions-advice.html

3   Weingarten, Laurie Kopp. "Should You Hire a College Consultant for Your Student?" CollegeXpress, 26 March 2019, https://www.collegexpress.com/counselors-and-parents/parents/blog/should-you-hire-college-consultant-your-student/.

the emerging college journey
- supporting your brood

If you are entering the world of the college journey, you may want to notice the connection with Brood X cicadas,[4] which are internally wired to wait for 17 years to emerge from underground, but when they emerge, they may find that the landscape has changed. It is a reminder of how even though the parents of 17 yr. olds have shared 17 years together; they bring vastly different perspectives to the college journey. While both may have been cocooned and evolving together for the last 17 years, parents bring history and adult skills that take years to develop, like prioritizing, decision-making, initiating tasks, and reflecting on lessons learned, all skills that help them see further down the road and manage their time and tasks. These types of skills take years of practice to hone and build and inevitably include missteps along the way. Most 17 yr. olds, however, are likely just beginning to work on these skills. While the mission of the Brood X cicadas is slightly different and constricted by time, the tasks of applying to college and supporting the goals of a 17 yr. old student also can be mission-focused.

What can parents do to support their high school student embarking on their college journey? ✓

- Give them space and time to explore colleges.

- Learn alongside them, and steel yourself from trying to take the lead.

- Let go of how college was when you attended 20+ years ago.

- Manage expectations.

- Learn from the experts.

- Enjoy the fun stuff like visiting colleges, finding the best food spots, or exploring local places.

When I think about helping students and families understand the college landscape, having the proper lens seems even more essential these days,

---

4 Trillions of cicadas are coming to the U.S. Here's why that's a good thing.
https://www.nationalgeographic.com/animals/article/brood-x-cicadas-actually-good-fear-not

as it will help focus the journey and the roles everyone plays. Unless a parent has worked in college admissions or higher education, their prior school and life experiences will be a huge part of the lens that will frame how they see the college landscape. As parents, the ability to look back on what their 20s were like often affirms lessons learned and what they valued most and may inform their aspirations for their high school student. Like the Brood X cicadas emerging after 17 years into a world unknown, parents may also see that the landscape of applying to college has changed significantly since they went to college.

step away from researching colleges on your teen's behalf.

You may have some good ideas of which schools may suit your high school student because, of course, you know them better than anyone, but ultimately it is your high school student who has to like the school, go to the school, navigate, and make their success unless you're planning on attending college with them.

step away from helping with the college essay.

Why? As hard it may be to wait or wonder if your rising senior is in the process of writing their college essays, this is a moment to sit on your hands. The process of thinking about what to write about, drafting, refining, and finalizing is not just an act of writing; it's also an opportunity to reflect, clarify and assert who they are to others. This is an opportunity to define or redefine themselves. When parents "help," they send the message that they don't believe their high school student is competent, that they are good enough, or that they can't get into college without parent assistance. Even worse, when admission decisions arrive, no matter which decision, it won't be a win. If the student doesn't get into a college, will the lingering question be because my parent helped too much with my essay and applications, or if they are admitted, does it mean the parent was accepted, not the student?

What else do parents need to help fine-tune what they're looking at as they watch their emerging 17-year-old pursue their college path?

trust the experts.

Find reliable resources[5] to help you understand what applying to college looks like now. Whether you have access to a college counselor at your high school, are working with a college counselor, or combing through books and online resources, aim to have the guidance be specific to your teen[6] based on their strengths, goals, and where they are in their educational path.

if you can't avert your eyes from rankings. reframe what you're looking at to see past the sheen of a ranking.

Understand what rankings[7] use as parameters to "rank" a school. You may be surprised that rankings have little to do with personalized student success. The better question to have is which school will give my student the skills and knowledge for success in the world, whether that includes soft skills, internship opportunities, hands-on learning, or access to professors. Let your high school student confirm by deep research what the academic program will be like, how strong alumni connections and career and internship programs are, and what businesses partner with each school and in what way. Give your high school student the time and space they need to start, stop and start again at their pace.

look at the overall cost to attend and graduate,

not just tuition per year early in the process. College Scorecard and each college's website have this information. Pair this using the Federal Student Aid Estimator[8] to get an idea of your (EFC) Expected Family Contribution. Understanding the difference between the cost of attending a public university versus a private college should include paying attention to the graduation rate. Finding out if a student can graduate in four years or will take longer translates directly to how

5 college.u LLC college.u LLC College Admission Resources, https://www.collegeu.solutions/collegeadmissionresources
6 Elizabeth Heaton, "Six Ways a College Counselor Counsels Her Own Son about Admissions," Grown and Flown, May 11, 2021
https://grownandflown.com/college-counselor-helps-son-college-application/
7 Paul Glastris and Grace Gedye, "A Different Kind of College Ranking" Washington Monthly, August 30, 2020 https://washingtonmonthly.com/2020/08/30/introduction-a-different-kind-of-college-ranking-11/
8 Federal Student Aid, FAFSA https://studentaid.gov/aid-estimator/#/landing

much it costs to attend college. Will it take longer to graduate from a public university because it will be harder to get classes? Does a public university offer an honors college that includes priority registration versus a private college where you can be done in four years? Do the math for the whole pie, not just tuition for each year, to see the differential between private and public schools.

Starting the college journey may evoke memories for parents of what it was like to be an emerging 17 yr. old, and will inevitably lead to thinking about different college experiences that are available, the opportunity to attend an alma mater, whether a gap year makes sense, and what employment or service opportunities may be pursued before starting college. All of these can be deeply personal and can lead to meaningful discussions as a family. Ultimately, letting students lead the way as they seek out their college path and emerge into adulthood will provide experiences that will translate to self-agency and self-advocacy skills, some of the many essential tools needed beyond the college journey. Having the correct lens will help everyone see the path ahead.

top 21 empty nest things to do

Years before my kids graduated from high school, a friend shared the best advice for when your children fly the coop: plan vacations that will make it impossible for them to turn down the invitation. While it may sound like an enticement, my friend's message reminded me that shared family experiences, whether they involve lost luggage, bungee jumping, or sitting on a beach, are sustaining and reaffirming and as valuable as laughter and traditions cultivated when everyone lived under one roof. Advice from friends is a good starting point for soon-to-be empty nesters, and recognizing this has nudged me to develop my own tips for friends, parents, and families about to transition to an empty nest. Not quite an empty-nester, but it's on the horizon? Still in the college-search mode? It's okay to look ahead and envision this part of the road so you have a good plan in place.

The empty nest checklist:

- Take back all the phone chargers in the house.
- Dine with friends at places that don't involve bringing snacks and sports drinks.
- Travel - in the off-season (no more staying home because of a try-out or team practice).
- KonMari or Hygge your home.
- Sleep in - well, at least until you have to get up for work.
- See all Oscar Nominated films in the movie theater - before the Academy Awards.
- Have as many "date nights" as you want - no babysitter required.
- Throw away single socks.
- Take up glass-blowing, painting, or raising chickens.
- Box-up awards and certificates are to be held until needed or given to the rightful owner.
- Do laundry as needed - it won't take all day or the weekend.
- Consider giving the Costco card to one of your kids.
- Eat whatever you want at dinner.
- Join clubs and museums, train for a marathon, take a Barre fitness class, or practice yoga (say good-bye PTA, Scouts, and driving carpool).
- Have the car detailed and dispose of anything unrecognizable.
- Donate sportswear and gear to local groups or younger families in your neighborhood.
- Plan a fabulous trip for the entire family when college is out or on break.
- Step away from Facebook and enjoy face-to-face time.
- Create a recipe book of all your kids' favorite dishes. (If you want to give it as a gift, start well before the holidays. It will take longer than you think and may involve a box of Kleenex).
- Take back a bedroom or two with a small renovation or new paint - can you say home office, man cave, den, true guest room? Or perhaps some personal TLC and personal remodeling...
- Enjoy the stories of your children, friends' children, and community - everyone's journey will be unique and rich in spirit.

- CollegeAnswer
- College Scorecard
- CAL State East Bay Preview
- California Community Colleges
- Colleges That Change Lives
- Big Future, College Board
- California Colleges.edu
- The California State University
- University of California Schools
- The Common Application
- Coalition for College Access
- Campus Pride Strive for College
- Quest Bridge
- Posse Foundation
- I'm First Reach Higher | Better Make Room
- uAspire
- Point Foundation
- girls inc.
- 826 Valencia
- Beyond 12
- CTCL College Fairs
- NACAC College Fairs
- WACAC College Fairs
- National Portfolio Day

- The Parent's Guide to Filling Out the FAFSA® Form

- FAFSA Glossary - From the FAFSA website https://studentaid. ed.gov/sa/

- FAFSA- The office of Federal Student Aid provides grants, loans, and work-study funds for college or career school. FAFSA provides more than $120 billion in federal student aid annually to help pay for college or career school.

- CSS-Nearly 400 colleges, professional schools, and scholarship programs use CSS Profile to award nonfederal aid. UC Blue & Gold Plan The Blue and Gold Opportunity Plan is a financial aid program intended to expand access to UC for lower-income students.

- Cal Grants- "A Cal Grant is money for college you don't have to pay back. To qualify, you must apply for the Free Application for Federal Student Aid (FAFSA) or California Dream Act Application (CADAA) by the deadline and meet the eligibility and financial requirements and any minimum GPA requirements. Cal Grants can be used at any University of California, California State University, or California Community College, as well as qualifying independent and career colleges or technical schools in California." California Student Aid Commission.

- FAST Web • Scholarships.com An online search tool to find scholarships.

- MeritAid.com- An online scholarship search tool.

- Niche

- Search lists of scholarships by choosing a category or getting matched to college scholarships you are eligible for.

- UNCF - United Negro College Foundation

- Fund Hispanic Scholarship Fund

- APIA Scholars

- Coca-Cola Scholars Dell Scholars Program

"People take different roads seeking
fulfillment and happiness.
Just because they're not on your road
doesn't mean they've gotten lost."

~ Dalai Lama

books

"Read." It is my favorite word (other than "accepted.")[1] Being "well-read" provides an essential foundation for comprehension, critical thought, and communication. The amount of parenting and college admission books intended to help students and parents navigate the college journey may seem endless. Here, I share my favorites and must-have books. Look for seasonal "Recommended Reads" throughout the year on the college.u website and occasionally in newsletters.

[1] Read Patrick Sullivan, English Professor's "An Open Letter to High School Students about Reading" posted on Stanford University's Tomorrow's Professor Posting page.

For more book recommendations, visit the college.u books that guide.

....

Antonoff, Steven R. *College Match: A Blueprint for Choosing the Best School for You.* Steven R. Antonoff, 2022

Armstrong, Thomas. *The Power of Neurodiversity: Unleashing the Advantages of Your Differently Wired Brain* (published in Hardcover as Neurodiversity). Hachette Books, 2011

Bauld, Harry. *On Writing the College Application Essay, 25th Anniversary Edition: The Key to Acceptance at the College of Your Choice.* HarperCollins, 2012

Best Liberal Arts Colleges - More than 2020 College Rankings — the Complete Guide to Liberal Arts Colleges

Bruni, Frank. *Where You Go Is Not Who You'll Be: An Antidote to the College Admissions Mania.* Grand Central Publishing, 2016

Caplan, Carolyn. *hey admissionsmom: REAL TALK from reddit,* AdmissionsMom, LLC 2019

Clark, Rick, and Brennan Barnard. *The Truth about College Admission: A Family Guide to Getting In and Staying Together.* Johns Hopkins University Press, 2019

Coburn, Karen Levin, and Madge Lawrence Treeger. *Letting Go, Sixth Edition: A Parents' Guide to Understanding the College Years.* HarperCollins, 2016

Fields, Timothy L., and Shereem Herndon-Brown. *The Black Family's Guide to College Admissions: A Conversation about Education, Parenting, and Race.* Johns Hopkins University Press, 2022

Fiske, Edward. *Fiske Guide to Colleges 2023.* Sourcebooks, Incorporated, 2022

Gladwell, Malcolm. *David and Goliath: Underdogs, Misfits, and the Art of Battling Giants.* Little, Brown, 2015

Gladwell, Malcolm. *Lord of the Rankings.* no. Season 6, Episode 2, Revisionist History Podcast

Golden, Daniel. *The Price of Admission (Updated Edition): How America's Ruling Class Buys Its Way Into Elite Colleges--and Who Gets Left Outside the Gates.* Crown, 2007

Grant, Adam. *Think Again: The Power of Knowing What You Don't Know.* Penguin Publishing Group, 2021.

Hamblet, Elizabeth C. *From High School to College: Steps to Success for Students with Disabilities.* Council for Exceptional Children, 2017

Heffernan, Lisa, and Mary Dell Harrington. *Grown and Flown: How to Support Your Teen, Stay Close as a Family, and Raise Independent Adults.* Flatiron Books, 2020

Horn, Michael B., and Bob Moesta. *Choosing College: How to Make Better Learning Decisions Throughout Your Life.* Wiley, 2019

Hugo, Richard. *The Triggering Town: Lectures And Essays On Poetry And Writing.* WW Norton, 2010

Karabel, Jerome. *The Chosen: The Hidden History of Admission and Exclusion at Harvard, Yale, and Princeton*. Houghton Mifflin, 2005

Korn, Melissa, and Jennifer Levitz. *Unacceptable: Privilege, Deceit & the Making of the College Admissions Scandal*. Penguin Publishing Group, 2020

Lahey, Jessica. *The Gift of Failure: How the Best Parents Learn to Let Go So Their Children Can Succee*d. HarperCollins, 2016

Lemann, Nicholas. *The Big Test: The Secret History of the American Meritocracy*. Farrar, Straus and Giroux, 2000

Lieber, Ron. *The Price You Pay for College: An Entirely New Road Map for the Biggest Financial Decision Your Family Will Ever Make*. HarperCollins Publishers, 2022

Lythcott-Haims, Julie. *Your Turn: How to Be an Adult*. Henry Holt and Company, 2022.

Pope, Loren. *Colleges That Change Lives: 40 Schools That Will Change the Way You Think About Colleges.* Edited by Hilary Masell Oswald, Penguin Publishing Group, 2012

Robinson, Janine. Escape Essay Hell! A Step-By-Step Guide to Writing Narrative College Application Essays. CreateSpace Independent Publishing Platform, 2013

Sawyer, Ethan. *College Essay Essentials: A Step-By-Step Guide to Writing a Successful College Admission Essay*. Sourcebooks, Incorporated, 2016

Selingo, Jeffrey. *Who Gets In and Why: A Year Inside College Admissions*. Scribner, 2020.

Thurber, James. *"The Secret Life of Walter Mitty."* The New Yorker, 1939

Toor, Rachel. *Write Your Way In: Crafting an Unforgettable College Admissions Essay*. University of Chicago Press, 2017

Tough, Paul. *The Years that Matter Most: How College Makes Or Breaks Us*. Houghton Mifflin Harcourt, 2019

article citations

"College Programs." College Autism Spectrum, https://collegeautism-spectrum.com/collegeprograms/

"How Companies Are Increasing Neurodiversity in the Workplace." Knowledge at Wharton, 2019, https://knowledge.wharton.upenn.edu/podcast/knowledge-at-wharton-podcast/autism-employment/

"IPEDS " Integrated Postsecondary Education Data System NCES, https://nces.ed.gov/ipeds/

College Scorecard | College Scorecard, https://collegescorecard.ed.gov

Colleges That Change Lives – Changing Lives. One Student At A Time, https://ctcl.org

CollegeXpress: Scholarships, College Search, Lists and Rankings, https://www.collegexpress.com

Nyhan, Sean. "Disability or Divergent Characteristic: Inside the Neurodiversity Movement." NACA, Journal for College Admissions, 2018, https://knowledge.wharton.upenn.edu/podcast/knowledge-at-wharton-podcast/autism-employment/

Saks J.D., PhD., Elyn. The Factors for Living a Productive Life., https://www.youtube.com/watch?v=g0pFh6voMuI

"A Work in Progress: A Scholar's Story — The Center for Reintegration." *The Center for Reintegration*, 6 November 2019, https://www.reintegration.com/new-blog/2019/11/6/a-work-in-progress-a-scholars-story

"'Absolutely Shocked': California Teen Accepted To 5 Ivy League Schools And Stanford." APRIL 11, 2021, https://www.cbsnews.com/sanfrancisco/news/sylmar-teen-accepted-to-5-ivy-league-schools-and-stanford/

"8 Steps to Completing the FAFSA® Form – Federal Student Aid." *Federal Student Aid*, https://studentaid.gov/articles/steps-to-complete-fafsa-form/

"A Student's Guide To Your First Year of College." YouTube, 19 September 2019, https://www.youtube.com/playlist?list=PLVix8d69s-Pe4PZ5M0YCmgdqIcFmvGuMZ0

"Admission Consideration - Undergraduate Admission." Carnegie Mellon University, https://www.cmu.edu/admission/admission/admission-consideration

"Admissions index instructions." *UC Admissions*, https://admission.universityofcalifornia.edu/admission-requirements/freshman-requirements/california-residents/statewide-guarantee/admissions-index-instructions.html

"Application affirmations." Common App, https://www.commonapp.org/application-affirmations

"College Counseling - The Berkeley Carroll School." Berkeley Carroll School, https://www.berkeleycarroll.org/academics/college-counseling

"College Programs." College Autism Spectrum, https://collegeautismspectrum.com/collegeprograms/

"Doughnut Recipes & Menu Ideas | Bon Appétit." Bon Appetit, https://www.bonappetit.com/dish/doughnut

"FAFSA® Application Deadlines." *Federal Student Aid*, https://studentaid.gov/apply-for-aid/fafsa/fafsa-deadlines

"FAFSA® Application." *Federal Student Aid*, https://studentaid.gov/h/apply-for-aid/fafsa

"Federal Student Aid Estimator." *Federal Student Aid*, https://studentaid.gov/aid-estimator/

"Filling Out the FAFSA® Form." *Federal Student Aid*, https://studentaid.

gov/apply-for-aid/fafsa/filling-out?utm_source=twitter_fsa&utm_medium=social&utm_campaign=202223fafsa&utm_content=20210907.

"Filling Out the FAFSA® Form." *Federal Student Aid*, https://studentaid.gov/apply-for-aid/fafsa/filling-out#gathering-the-documents-needed-to-apply.

"Four Ways to Beat College Application Stress - UIUC Admissions Blog." UIUC Admissions Blog, 11 October 2022, https://blog.admissions.illinois.edu/four-ways-to-beat-college-application-stress/

"Freshman requirements | UC Admissions." UC Admissions, https://admission.universityofcalifornia.edu/admission-requirements/freshman-requirements/.

"Freshmen by the numbers | Office of Admissions." Office of Admissions, https://admit.washington.edu/apply/freshman/by-the-numbers/.

"Hey, UC grads: Could you get into your alma mater today?" KPCC, 23 March 2018, https://www.kpcc.org/news/2018/03/23/81849/hey-uc-grads-could-you-get-into-your-alma-mater-to/.

"How Companies Are Increasing Neurodiversity in the Workplace." Knowledge at Wharton, 2019, https://knowledge.wharton.upenn.edu/podcast/knowledge-at-wharton-podcast/autism-employment/.

"How to Renew Your FAFSA® Application." *Federal Student Aid*, https://studentaid.gov/apply-for-aid/fafsa/renew

"Impaction." Cal Poly, https://www.calpoly.edu/admissions/impaction.

"Postsecondary Education (College or University)." Autism Speaks, https://www.autismspeaks.org/postsecondary-education-college-or-university

"Postsecondary Education (College or University)." *Autism Speaks*, https://www.autismspeaks.org/postsecondary-education-college-or-university.

"Procrastination – The Writing Center • University of North Carolina at Chapel Hill." UNC Writing Center, https://writingcenter.unc.edu/tips-and-tools/procrastination/

"Save On College Tuition | Western Undergraduate Exchange (WUE)."

WICHE, https://www.wiche.edu/tuition-savings/wue/.

"Standardized Testing and Students with Disabilities." Fairtest, 2017. Fairtest, https://fairtest.org/standardized-testing-and-students-disabilities/

"The College Essay: Tips to Build the Best 'Story of You.'" Ursinus College, https://www.ursinus.edu/admission/starting-the-college-search/the-college-essay-tips-to-build-the-best-story-of-you/

"The Learning Effectiveness Program | Student Affairs." DU Student Affairs, https://studentaffairs.du.edu/learningeffectiveness.

"Ugh, I Have to Write Another Essay? – Colleges That Change Lives." Colleges That Change Lives, https://ctcl.org/ugh-i-have-to-write-another-essay/

"UMich 101: New Student Survival Guide - Office of Undergraduate Admissions." University of Michigan Admissions, https://admissions.mivideo.it.umich.edu/playlist/dedicated/190098433/1_23bm-43wb/1_1uabq5al.

"Understanding the FAFSA® Process for Parents – *Federal Student Aid*." Federal Student Aid, https://studentaid.gov/articles/parents-understanding-fafsa/.

"Volunteer." Oakland Public Library, 16 February 2023, https://oaklandlibrary.org/volunteer/

"What is my Expected Family Contribution (EFC)?" *Federal Student Aid*, https://studentaid.gov/help-center/answers/article/what-is-efc

Abrams, Tanya. "Tip Sheet: If You Are Accepted, Rejected or Deferred." New York Times, 27 March 2013, https://archive.nytimes.com/thechoice.blogs.nytimes.com/2013/03/27/tip-sheet-if-you-are-accepted-rejected-or-deferred/

Active Minds - Changing the conversation about mental health, https://www.activeminds.org.

ADA.gov: The Americans with Disabilities Act, https://www.ada.gov.

Applerouth PhD, Jed. "Affluence and Accommodations: Wealthier

Students are Securing More School-based Accommodations for Disabilities." August 13, 2019. applerouth, https://www.applerouth.com/blog/2019/08/13/affluence-and-accommodations-wealthier-students-are-securing-more-school-based-accommodations-for-disabilities/

Barnard, Brennan. "New Research Finds That Character Counts In College Admission." Forbes, 2020, https://www.forbes.com/sites/brennanbarnard/2020/02/13/new-research-finds-that-character-counts-in-college-admission/?sh=1efd97907475

Barnard, Brennan. "The College Admission Blind Taste Test." Forbes, 2018, https://www.forbes.com/sites/brennanbarnard/2018/08/08/the-college-admission-blind-taste-test/?sh=133ea73b6ecd

Barnard, Brennan. "The Royal "We" in College Admission." 2018. Forbes, https://www.forbes.com/sites/brennanbarnard/2018/05/25/the-royal-we-in-college-admission/?sh=4bc4be5d4fbd

Barnes, Erin. "FAFSA & CSS Profile - A Straightforward Guide to Understanding Financial Aid." *SCOIR*, https://www.scoir.com/blog/fafsa-css-profile-a-straightforward-guide.

Bauer, Jeremy. "Common App: Applications to highly selective colleges up by 25% in 2 years." Higher Ed Dive, 28 February 2022, https://www.highereddive.com/news/common-app-applications-to-highly-selective-colleges-up-by-25-in-2-years/619529/

Belkin, Douglas. "Colleges Mine Data on Their Applicants - WSJ." The Wall Street Journal, 26 January 2019, https://www.wsj.com/articles/the-data-colleges-collect-on-applicants-11548507602

Berler, Nina. "In College Admissions, Is It Important To Show Your Love?" 2019. Forbes, https://www.forbes.com/sites/noodleeducation/2019/02/14/in-college-admissions-is-it-important-to-show-your-love/?sh=48b9d2112058

Best Liberal Arts Colleges - More than 2020 College Rankings — the Complete Guide to Liberal Arts Colleges, https://www.liberalartscolleges.com

Better Make Room: Home, https://www.bettermakeroom.org

Bittman, Mark. "Doughnuts Recipe - NYT Cooking." NYT Cooking, https://cooking.nytimes.com/recipes/1017060-doughnuts

Boeckenstedt, Jon. Higher Ed Data Stories, https://www.highered-datastories.com/

Brad, Stulberg. "The Truth About Routines." Outside, 2020, https://www.outsideonline.com/health/training-performance/truth-about-routines/

Brenoff, Ann. "6 Things You Should Never Do As the Parent of a College Applicant." Huffpost, 2015, https://www.huffpost.com/entry/tk-mistakes-parents-make-when-they-help-kids-apply-to-college_n_55c-8b9ace4b0f73b20b9e928

Bring Change to Mind - Let's Talk Mental Health, https://bringchange2mind.org

Caldwell, Tanya. "6 Tips About College Admissions Results - The New York Times." The New York Times Web Archive, 30 March 2012, https://archive.nytimes.com/thechoice.blogs.nytimes.com/2012/03/30/6-tips-about-college-admissions-results/

Cao, Melissa. "Let's talk about interviews." MIT Admissions, 24 October 2022, https://mitadmissions.org/blogs/entry/lets-talk-about-interviews/

Carrns, Ann. "More States Require High School Seniors to Fill Out Financial Aid Form." The New York Times, 14 October 2022, https://www.nytimes.com/2022/10/14/your-money/states-fafsa.html.

Clark, Rick. "Change is the Only Constant." Georgia Tech Admission Blog, 20 March 2020, https://sites.gatech.edu/admission-blog/2020/03/20/change-is-the-only-constant/

Clark, Rick. "Rick Clark (@Clark2College)." Twitter, https://twitter.com/Clark2College.

Clark, Rick. "The Waitlist. Why?!" Georgia Tech Admission Blog, 23 March 2021, https://sites.gatech.edu/admission-blog/2021/03/23/the-waitlist-why/

Cole, Jonathan R. "Why Sports and Elite Academics Do Not Mix." The Atlantic, 2017, https://www.theatlantic.com/education/archive/2017/03/the-case-against-student-athletes/518739/

College Database Find the Best Colleges in US | CollegeData, https://www.collegedata.com.

College Disability Accommodations Information - Elizabeth C. Hamblet, https://ldadvisory.com.

College Scorecard | College Scorecard, https://collegescorecard.ed.gov

Colleges That Change Lives – Changing Lives. One Student At A Time, https://ctcl.org

CollegeXpress: Scholarships, College Search, Lists and Rankings, https://www.collegexpress.com

CSS Profile – *CSS Profile*, https://cssprofile.collegeboard.org.

Curran, David. "Want to play college sports? Here are your best chances." SFGATE, 19 November 2017, https://www.sfgate.com/sports/article/Good-sports-for-your-kid-to-get-a-college-12354371.php#photo-10718738

Depression and Bipolar Support Alliance: DBSA, https://www.dbsalliance.org

Dix, Willard. "Plan Ahead To Be College Eligible.", https://www.forbes.com/sites/willarddix/2017/07/31/plan-ahead-to-be-college-eligible/?sh=5eab1a92fbfe

Dix, Willard. "Tell Colleges You Love Them." Forbes, 2017, https://www.forbes.com/sites/willarddix/2017/09/06/tell-colleges-you-love-them/?sh=4f9de9291de7

Dix, Willard. "You Need to Understand Your Educational Rights." Forbes, 2018, https://www.forbes.com/sites/willarddix/2018/05/16/you-need-to-understand-your-educational-privacy-rights/?sh=128212736b93

Dix, Willard. Pros and Cons of Strategizing for College. Forbes Magazine, https://www.forbes.com/sites/willarddix/2016/06/28/pros-and-cons-of-strategizing-for-college/?sh=fec1b6c3fddc

Fletcher, Christine. "What Legal Documents Do Your Kids Need Before Going To College?" Forbes, 29 August 2018, https://www.forbes.com/

sites/christinefletcher/2018/08/29/what-legal-documents-do-your-kids-need-before-going-to-college/?sh=4c9cb8654ca4.

Food is a basic human right. Help us end hunger in the bay Area., 5 October 2022, https://www.accfb.org

Freedberg, Louis. "California's public universities struggle with rising college eligibility." EdSource, 17 August 2017, https://edsource. org/2017/californias-public-universities-struggle-with-rising-college-eligibility /585841.

Freidus, Andrea. "The problem with volunteer tourism for NGOs is it doesn't do much good." Quartz, 2017,

https://qz.com/1124920/voluntourism-ngo-volunteers-turned-tourists-are-a-problem-in-africa

Geoff, Brumfiel. "Common Interpretation of Heisenberg's Uncertainty Principle Is Proved False." Scientific American, 2012,

 https://www.scientificamerican.com/article/common-interpretation-of-heisenbergs-uncertainty-principle-is-proven-false/

Glatter, Hayley. "The March Madness Application Bump." The Atlantic, 2017, https://www.theatlantic.com/education/archive/2017/03/the-march-madness-application-bump/519846/

GradGuard | College Life Protected, https://gradguard.com

Griffe, Susannah L. "Protecting Friendships During the College Admissions Process." New York Times, 5 December 2011, https://archive. nytimes.com/thechoice.blogs.nytimes.com/2011/12/05/friendship/

Grove, Allan. "Reach School in College Admissions." ThoughtCo., 2019 https://www.thoughtco.com/what-is-a-reach-school-788442.

Helhoski, Anna, and Des Toups. "What is Need-Based Financial Aid?" *NerdWallet*, 15 June 2022, https://www.nerdwallet.com/article/loans/student-loans/need-and-merit-based-financial-aid.

Herrera, Tim. "8 Ways to Better Navigate the Internet in 2020." The New York Times, 26 December 2019, https://www.nytimes.

com/2019/12/26/smarter-living/internet-etiquette-data-privacy-cleanse-digital-tracking.html

Hertzberg, Karen. "How to Write the Perfect Thank You Letter." Grammarly, 13 May 2019, https://www.grammarly.com/blog/how-to-write-a-thank-you-letter/

Home | NAMI: National Alliance on Mental Illness, https://www.nami.org/Home

Why Sports and Elite Academics Do Not Mix, The Atlantic, March 2017, https://www.theatlantic.com/education/archive/2017/03/the-case-against-student-athletes/518739/

Jacobs, Peter. "Ronald Nelson Turned Down Every Ivy League School for University of Alabama." Business Insider, 14 May 2015, https://www.businessinsider.com/ronald-nelson-turned-down-every-ivy-league-school-for-university-of-alabama-2015-5

Jeffrey, Selingo. "What Vanderbilt, Northwestern and other elite colleges don't say about acceptance rates." The Washington Post, October 7, 2017, https://www.washingtonpost.com/news/grade-point/wp/2017/10/07/what-vanderbilt-northwestern-and-other-elite-colleges-dont-say-about-acceptance-rates/

Kantrowitz, Mark. "How FAFSA Simplification Will Change Financial Aid Eligibility." *Saving for College*, https://www.savingforcollege.com/article/how-fafsa-simplification-will-change-financial-aid-eligibility

Korn, Melissa, and Anne Tergesen. "College Admissions Group Votes to Allow More Aggressive Student Recruiting." Wall Street Journal, 28 September 2019, https://www.wsj.com/articles/college-admissions-group-votes-to-allow-more-aggressive-student-recruiting-11569701995

Koubek, Christine. "Tired of people asking where you're going to college? Here's what to say." *The Washington Post*, 23 February 2017, https://www.washingtonpost.com/lifestyle/magazine/the-most-annoying-question-high-school-seniors-get-and-how-to-deal/2017/02/22/955da1e0-e17a-11e6-a547-5fb9411d332c_story.html?postshare=5371488133060669&tid=ss_tw-bottom&utm_term=.429db9719326

Kristof, Nicholas. "Opinion | The Four Secrets of Success." *The New York Times*, 7 December 2019, https://www.nytimes.com/2019/12/07/opinion/sunday/student-success-advice.html?smid=nytcore-ios-share

Leonard, Ben, et al. "Three Critical Legal Documents Every Parent of a College Student Should Get in Place As Soon As Possible." National Law Review, 26 September 2017, https://www.natlawreview.com/article/three-critical-legal-documents-every-parent-college-student-should-get-place-soon

Malcolm, Gladwell. Why Did I say "Yes" to Speak Here. Elite Institutional Cognitive Disorder., https://www.youtube.com/watch?v=3UEwbRWFZVc

Mchale Dangremond, Meghan. "While You're Waiting." Tufts Blog, https://admissions.tufts.edu/blogs/inside-admissions/post/while-youre-waiting/

Merrill, Martha C. "A Dean's Advice to Seniors: Don't Slack Off." New York Times, 6 February 2012, https://archive.nytimes.com/thechoice.blogs.nytimes.com/2012/02/06/dont-slack-off/

Milaschewski, Dan. "My Very Unofficial Tips on Writing Your College Essay." Harvard College Blog, 2016, https://college.harvard.edu/student-life/student-stories/my-very-unofficial-tips-writing-your-college-essay

Mission Blue: Home, https://missionblue.org

NaNoWriMo: Welcome, https://nanowrimo.org

Nyhan, Sean. "Disability or Divergent Characteristic: Inside the Neurodiversity Movement." NACA, Journal for College Admissions, 2018, https://read.nxtbook.com/nacac/the_journal_of_college_admiss/fall_2018/neurodiverse_students.html.

Pisana, Gary P. "Neurodiversity as a Competitive Advantage." Harvard Business Review, 2017, https://hbr.org/2017/05/neurodiversity-as-a-competitive-advantage

Pope, Devin, and Jaren Pope. "Colleges receive more applications when their basketball teams do well." Economist, 2018, https://www.economist.com/graphic-detail/2018/03/26/colleges-receive-more-applications-when-their-basketball-teams-do-well

Reed, Matt. "Demonstrated Interest' Is Really Time-Consuming." Inside Higher Ed, 2018, https://www.insidehighered.com/blogs/confessions-community-college-dean/demonstrated-interest-really-time-consuming

Saks J.D., PhD., Elyn. The Factors for Living a Productive Life., https://www.youtube.com/watch?v=g0pFh6voMuI.

SALT Center: Welcome, https://www.salt.arizona.edu

Sawyer, Art. "ACT Announces Section Retesting, Superscore Reporting, and Online Testing." 2019. Compass Education Group, https://www.compassprep.com/act-section-retesting/

Schiffman, Jeff. "How to Stay Admitted." Tulane University Admission Blog - Jeff Schiffman, 12 January 2021, http://tuadmissionjeff.blogspot.com/2020/01/how-to-stay-admitted.html

Schiffman, Jeff. "So You're Using a College Counselor." Tulane University Admission Blog, 11 January 2019, http://tuadmissionjeff.blogspot.com/2018/01/so-youre-using-independent-counselor.html?view=timeslide

Schworm, Peter. "College applications can be too good - The Boston Globe." Boston.com, 12 February 2008, http://archive.boston.com/news/education/higher/articles/2008/02/12/college_applications_can_be_too_good/

Steiner, Matty. "Accommodations Requests: SAT vs. ACT." Compass Education Group, July 1, 2022, https://www.compassprep.com/accommodations-requests-sat-vs-act/

Stiller, Ben. "The Secret Life Of Walter Mitty - Trailer #1." YouTube, 31 July 2013, https://www.youtube.com/watch?v=kGWO2w0H2V8.

Toor, Rachel. "Hearing the Voice of a 51-Year-Old Man in the Essay of a 17-Year-Old Girl." The New York Times Web Archive, 19 October 2010, https://archive.nytimes.com/thechoice.blogs.nytimes.com/2010/10/19/toor/

Tracy, Marc. "How College Sports Killed Summer Vacation." The New York Times, 31 July 2018, https://www.nytimes.com/2018/07/31/sports/college-sports-summer.html

Tretina, Kat. "What Is The Student Aid Index? – Forbes Advisor." *Forbes*, 21 April 2021, https://www.forbes.com/advisor/student-loans/what-is-the-student-aid-index/.

Truong, Debbie, et al. "How UC, CSU prepare for active shooters." Los Angeles Times, 15 February 2023, https://www.latimes.com/california/story/2023-02-15/how-californias-colleges-are-prepared-for-active-shooters-in-wake-of-michigan-state

turn-it-in.com, http://turn-it-in.com

Watanabe, Teresa. "UC Berkeley may be forced by court to cut 3000 undergraduate seats, freeze enrollment." Los Angeles Times, 15 February 2022, https://www.latimes.com/california/story/2022-02-14/uc-berkeley-may-be-forced-to-cut-3-000-freshman-seats-under-court-order-to-halt-growth

Watanabe, Teresa. "UC record college admission applications show wide diversity." Los Angeles Times, 29 January 2021, https://www.latimes.com/california/story/2021-01-29/uc-record-college-admission-applications-show-wide-diversity

Wichard-Edds, Adrienne. "Experts offer four reasons why kids need to own their own essays- and one-way parents can help." Washington Post, 13 October 2020, https://www.washingtonpost.com/lifestyle/2020/10/13/college-essay-advice/

Wolf, Nancy L. "Evaluating Mental Health Support of a College." Road2College, 25 March 2022, https://www.road2college.com/dont-ignore-mental-health-services-when-evaluating-colleges/

For more resources and information,
visit the college.u website at https://www.collegeu.solutions

online resources

Active Minds | https://www.activeminds.org

Additude Magazine | https://www.additudemag.com/best-journals-planners-adhd-time-management/

Alameda County Food Bank | https://www.accfb.org

AmeriCorps | https://americorps.gov

American Institute for Learning and Human Development | https://www.institute4learning.com/resources/articles/neurodiversity/

Americans with Disabilities Act-ADA.gov | https://www.ada.gov.

AMIGOS- Volunteer Abroad for Teens in Latin America | https://amigosinternational.org

APIA Scholars | https://apiascholars.org

Autism Speaks | https://www.autismspeaks.org/postsecondary-education-college-or-university

Bay Area Youth Agency | https://www.bayac.org

Better Make Room: Home | https://www.bettermakeroom.org

Beyond 12 | https://www.beyond12.org

Big Future, College Board | https://bigfuture.collegeboard.org

Bittman, Mark. "Doughnuts Recipe - NYT Cooking." NYT Cooking-https://cooking.nytimes.com/recipes/1017060-doughnuts.

Boeckenstedt, Jon. Higher Ed Data Stories | https://www.highered-datastories.com/

Bon Appetit-Doughnut Recipes & Menu Ideas | Bon Appétit | https://www.bonappetit.com/dish/doughnut

Bring Change to Mind - Let's Talk Mental Health | https://bringchange2mind.org

Cal Grants | https://www.csac.ca.gov/cal-grants

CAL State East Bay Preview | https://www.csueastbay.edu/preview-day/

California Colleges.edu | https://www.californiacolleges.edu/#/

California Community Colleges | https://www.cccco.edu/Students

California State University | https://www.calstate.edu/apply

Campus Pride Strive for College | https://www.campuspride.org

Cappex | https://www.cappex.com/scholarships

Center for Reintegration | https://www.reintegration.com/

Challenge Success | https://challengesuccess.org

Coalition for College Access | https://www.coalitionforcollegeaccess.org

Coca-Cola Scholars Dell Scholars Program | https://www.coca-cola-scholarsfoundation.org/

College Autism Spectrum - College Programs | https://collegeautism-spectrum.com/collegeprograms/

College Scorecard | https://collegescorecard.ed.gov

CollegeData | https://www.collegedata.com.

Colleges That Change Lives | https://ctcl.org

CollegeXpress | https://www.collegexpress.com

Common Application | https://www.commonapp.org

CSS Profile | https://cssprofile.collegeboard.org

CTCL College Fairs | https://ctcl.org/info-sessions/

Depression and Bipolar Support Alliance: DBSA | https://www.dbsalliance.org

FAFSA - Federal Student Aid | https://studentaid.gov/h/apply-for-aid/fafsa

FAFSA -Federal Student Aid Estimator | https://studentaid.gov/aid-estimator/#/landing

FAFSA Glossary | https://studentaid.ed.gov/sa/

Fastweb | https://www.fastweb.com

Federal Student Aid Estimator." Federal Student Aid | https://studentaid.gov/aid-estimator/

Forest | https://www.forestapp.cc

Gap Year Association | https://www.gapyearassociation.org/

girls inc. | https://girlsinc.org

Global Citizen Year: Global Gap Year Program | https://www.globalcitizenyear.org.

GradGuard | College Life Pro | https://gradguard.com.

Hispanic Scholarship Fund | https://www.hsf.net

IPEDS -Integrated Postsecondary Education Data System NCES | https://nces.ed.gov/ipeds/

Livescribe | https://us.livescribe.com

Mission Blue: Home | https://missionblue.org

NACAC College Fairs | https://www.nacacnet.org/nacac-college-fairs/

NAMI: National Alliance on Mental Illness | https://www.nami.org/Home

NaNoWriMo: Welcome | https://nanowrimo.org

National Portfolio Day | https://nationalportfolioday.org

Niche | https://www.niche.com

Notion | https://www.notion.so

Oakland Public Library -Volunteer | https://oaklandlibrary.org/volunteer/

Point Foundation | https://pointfoundation.org

Posse Foundation | https://www.possefoundation.org

Quest Bridge | https://www.questbridge.org

Reach Higher | https://www.bettermakeroom.org/reachhigher/

reMarkable | https://remarkable.com

SALT Center: Welcome | https://www.salt.arizona.edu

stickk | https://www.stickk.com

TeenLife | Experiential Learning | https://www.teenlife.com

uAspire | https://www.uaspire.org

UNCF - United Negro College Foundation | https://uncf.org

University of California Schools | https://admission.universityofcali
fornia.edu

WACAC College Fairs | https://www.wacac.org/college-fairs/wa-
cac-fairs/

Western Undergraduate Exchange (WUE) -Save On College Tuition |
https://www.wiche.edu/tuition-savings/wue/

Where There Be Dragons - Gap Year Programs | Africa, Asia, America,
Nepal, China | Dragons | https://www.wheretherebedragons.com/
students/find-your-adventure/gap-year/

WICHE -Welcome to Your WUE Savings Finder. | https://www.
wiche.edu/tuition-savings/wue/wue-savings-finder/

Wrightslaw Special Education Law and Advocacy | https://www.
wrightslaw.com

Youth Conservation Corps (YCC) | https://www.youthconservation-
corps.org

826 Valencia | https://826valencia.org

acknowledgments

While it may seem cliché to hear, "It takes a village," the reality is that no one truly goes through their college journey or life alone, whether it is families supporting their kids, teachers supporting their students, or counselors supporting everyone. I am forever grateful to my supporters, my husband with an open heart and ears, and my partner in crime, who sees the best parts in me and shares belly laughs when levity is most needed. Marna, who patiently let me think through what was most important, and my friend Heidi, taking turns finishing sentences with an unspoken bond. Sandra could translate my words into images that clarified what I wanted to convey. Brooke and Connie opened the door to foundational work experiences that helped me refine the best ways to support students. My parents inspired tenacity and shared the joy of reading. And most importantly, my kids, who raised me to see them as amazing, evolving humans that make my life richer by being invited into their journeys.

This book wouldn't have been possible without the students and families who invited me into their lives to help them carry their dreams forward. I am beyond grateful for the opportunity to witness the transformational process for high school students and the deep learning that has come from my work with colleagues, teachers, and mentors. I feel bolstered and in awe by the admission and higher education experts championing students and access to education and the writers and journalists who give voice to the unspoken truths. The gifts from supporting the future of others have been instrumental to my hunger to learn and improve. Had I known learning about rocket fuel, the perfect chocolate cake recipe, or how to pick a watermelon would bring such joy, I certainly would have started sooner. Nothing can be better than changing the world one student at a time and affirming that no two students are alike and no two paths the same.

about the author

d ane copeland is the Founder of college.u L.L.C., a private
college consulting practice supporting students and families on
their college journey. She has a College Counseling Certificate with
Distinction from UCLA, a B.A. in Psychology from the University
of Michigan, and an M.F.A. in Creative Writing. She lives in the
Bay Area with her husband and beloved "empty nest" pup and loves
spending time with her children.